MW01121212

Stay FIERCE !
Tamara.

Forgiveness and Other ~~Stupid~~ Things

An Awakening That Was Written in the Scars

TAMARA PLANT

.

Copyright © 2015 Tamara Plant

All rights reserved.

ISBN-13: 978-1517789985

DEDICATION

I only get one shot at a first book dedication so bear with me.

This book has been a lifetime work-in-progress but I only started to seriously develop it in 2013, when I was 38. As I write this, I'm a couple of weeks into my 40th year and have never felt more complete and ready to immerse myself in the rest of this journey. I believe this is where it gets really good for me.

I am dedicating this book to everyone who has come in and out of my life for the past 40 years, good or bad, because you have all taught me something, regardless of whether I wanted you in my life or not. I would not be the person I am if you had not touched my life in some way, shape or form so thank you for coming into my life.

My grandparents have been the two most influential people in my life and I will forever be grateful to them for teaching me that I could be anything I wanted to and to treat everyone, regardless of age, race, religion or status, with respect.

I have a handful of friends I need to thank for being there throughout the years even when they didn't understand the journey I was on. You know who you are.

This might seem strange but I need to thank Eminem. I swear to God his *Recovery* album spoke to me in a way that no one and nothing else could. I listened over and over to his lyrics about redemption, relapse and resilience. I can't thank him enough for his honesty about his story and inspiring me to share my own.

I am inspired every day by my daughter, Lauryn, who has taught me to be FIERCE in every aspect of my life. I named her after my grandma because I never knew a more beautiful soul than she was. Lauryn shines, smiles and sees the beauty in every person she meets just like my grandma did. She has the softest heart and the strongest spirit. I am beyond grateful that my littlest soulmate chose me to be her mom.

My compassionate, peaceful son, Oscar, has taught me that life doesn't have to be a boxing ring. I often wonder where he came from but know that he came to me to teach me that the world doesn't have to be full of anger, chaos or pain. Every time the damn kid sees me, he says, "I love you," and it's the most bizarre thing to me. I love him but he has this incessant need to say it and it's almost as though I'm being rewarded by the universe through him for the childhood I had.

Without the support of my amazingly understanding and forgiving husband, Ron, I wouldn't be where I am today. His quiet strength has gotten me through the darkest times, and I am beyond thankful for him even though I am the worst person at showing it. He never gave up on me even though I've given him a million reasons to walk away. The world needs more men like the man that he is and I thank my lucky stars every day that he is in my life.

Blah, blah, blah, enough with the sentimental shit. Let's get down to the good stuff!

Cheers!

tamara

CONTENTS

ACKNOWLEDGMENTS

Thanks to my editor, Kim Tannas, for placing the commas in the right places and cleaning up this content.

I don't have a lot of role models or mentors but a few have come into my life and I need to thank them for helping me become the person I am: Ruth Kelly for your continued belief in me, my father-in-law for understanding me and accepting me, dirty jokes and all (RIP Pops, I miss you), and everyone on Twitter who said I should take what I was saying and put it into a book.

In the end, I couldn't have written this story without my mom.

BEFORE YOU BEGIN YOU SHOULD KNOW THIS

I used to think the story I'm about to tell was my story but I've come to realize that it's also about the people who have come in and out of my life and have taught me who I am and who I don't want to be.

This is a book about forgiveness, enlightenment, detachment, resilience, transformation and a little bit of spirituality thrown in for good measure. These are all concepts I used to think were really stupid and signs of weakness. In reality, these lessons became like little shooting stars of salvation that I grabbed onto, clinging for dear life until I was ready to grab the next star of ascension and dive deep into the lessons I was meant to learn. Each of these stars brought me to this very moment; here with you and about to reach out and hand you one of these shining lessons.

Take one and see where it takes you. As I've discovered, you might not think these lessons are so stupid after all.

Don't be fooled by fancy terms like "enlightenment" or "spirituality." The stories and examples I give you will unapologetically show you who I was at my darkest and give you an uncensored look at myself, the people in my life and the twisted path I took to get here.

There was a time, not long ago, when I would see messages on social media from people spouting various forms of "inspiration" and uplifting quotes and think, "What a bunch of shit." I would sneer my disdain and roll my eyes at their cringe-worthy mantras that seemed so hokey and empty, so full of themselves with their pompously fake smiles and pretentious enlightenment.

I seriously. Fucking. Hated. Everything. And everyone. Especially myself, even if I didn't realize it at the time.

I mean if you're not Wayne Dyer or Louise Hay, just shut the fuck up already, I thought. How could anyone except a spiritual master like Deepak Chopra or Paulo Coelho claim to be enlightened when there was no way anyone could be that at peace with themselves? What had they ever gone through to make them so holier-than-thou? What made them so forgiving or at peace with their life, or some sort of expert on resilience? No way would they be able to tell ME that forgiveness was the key to inner peace when clearly there was no WAY they would be able to forgive if they were in my shoes. And who the hell were THEY, anyway? Who were they to tell me to let go? Who was anyone to suggest that by forgiving the people who caused me the most emotional, physical and spiritual damage, I would be better off?

They were idiots, I concluded. They had no idea.

That was the resentment I carried around with me for almost all of my 40 years on this Earth. It was deep-seated and ingrained in every breath I took and every suspicious stare I gave to almost anyone I came into contact with.

It wasn't all sandpaper and venom, though. I had moments where my true personality would shine through with joy, love, compassion, trust and an intense passion for life that led me to the greatest achievements I've enjoyed so far. But for the most part, I was swallowed up by the negativity which coloured my experiences; I allowed the darkness to define who I was.

In 2010, around the time I had tunnelled my way beneath rock bottom, I came across a couple of quotes by spirituality author Marianne Williamson that smacked me in the face with all kinds of truth.

Some of her most famous quotes, and my favourite aha moments, speak of how we are more comfortable in the darkness because being in the light exposes everything we are to the world. In the dark, we can hide in the shadows and wither away. In the light, we bloom and ascend closer to Source (that's geeky spiritual speak for God, creator, or whichever higher power you choose to follow). Which do you think most people choose? Well, for the longest time, I chose to wilt in the darkness.

I'd read her passages over and over and think, "Yeah whatever, Marianne," wiping away the tears of inadequacy and self-loathing. You don't know shit, Marianne, I said, grabbing tissues and rereading the verses.

Who was I to think I deserved anything good in my life? I mean, history dictated that every time I allowed myself a moment of happiness, something big and bad would come along and destroy any sense of security I had. I wasn't "shrinking" or afraid of my darkness, Marianne! I sniffled and wiped more tears thinking about how hardcore and badass as I was. I was used to protecting myself and retreating to survival mode because it was what I knew.

Survival instincts, after all, are what got me through my childhood and even though I was YEARS away from being a kid, the demons that followed me throughout my life were still very much haunting me as an adult.

Looking in the mirror, I hated who I had become and often wondered where the vibrant, flirty, sassy young girl had gone. My reflection showed a very broken version of my former self, and I wondered what it would take to put those pieces back together, if only for a moment, so that I could prove to myself that I wasn't who I had become. I missed the 21-year-old me. She was so alive and sure of herself. She was fearless and certain of her path in life. The 35-year-old me was insecure and unsure of herself, second-guessing the choices she had made and sabotaging the life she was living.

I didn't know how to pick up the pieces or where to start but I knew things had to change. I looked for messages anywhere and everywhere, trying to figure out the best way to patch myself back together and found them in the oddest of places: Twitter, Facebook, my angels and Eminem became conduits to a message I needed to hear. Yes, Eminem. Look, I'm not your typical spirit junkie. Eminem's resilience and raw lyrics speak to me in a way that the words of the most profound Zen teachers do not.

Thanks to these messages, a lot of hard work and some intense transformation, I've learned to let go of the past. I definitely don't hold onto the pain I experienced or the losses I have suffered because I know there are millions of other people who have suffered the same or worse.

I'm grateful to finally be at a point in my life where I'm strong enough to share everything and that I can take the opportunity to offer some insight into who I am and why I've decided to live a FIERCE life.

Do not take my advice as a replacement for professional help. I am not educated as a psychologist, life coach or psychiatrist. I have simply overcome the roadblocks and detours along the way on my life's journey and am sharing the way I've survived, crashed and burned, pulled myself up, fallen back down, given up on myself but ultimately risen up from the ashes of my life, time and time again.

As a thank you, I've added a bonus chapter and created a workbook which you can find on YouAreFIERCE.com/TheBook. I'm sharing this story to inspire you to keep going no matter what the universe throws your way or how bad things seem. In order to break through some of your own barriers, you need to do the work. This is my journey, so take from it what you need and implement it into your own life. You might not agree with everything and that's OK. You need to make your own life great, not emulate someone else's existence.

Inspiration doesn't have to come wrapped up in a cute little package filled with wonder and awe; sometimes it comes with a kick in the ass and an f-bomb or six so buckle up and enjoy the ride!

THE JOURNEY BEGINS

We're all given a life, regardless of how we believe we entered it: bad luck, past life karma, reincarnation, or dropped off by a stork.

You're born and you will die. It's what you do in between that time, whose lives you affect and the differences you make in the lives of others that matter the most because when you're gone, your memory and what you leave behind will have touched the heart and souls of other people.

Life begins and so does your journey but it's the people who cross your path, walk with you or stand in your way that teach you the greatest lessons and shape your story while you're on this Earth.

My story started with my mom, so let's begin there.

She was 18 when she got pregnant with me in 1974 which, I was told, was frowned upon back then.

When I was about six years old, I started to question her about who my dad was and what it was like when she had me, needing to have some knowledge of who I really was and how my journey began.

Lighting a cigarette, she looked at me across the kitchen

table and I could see her thinking about how to answer my questions. Instead of censoring herself, she answered the way she answered everything else. Bluntly and without a filter.

"So one day I was out and I heard this awful crying. I couldn't figure out where it came from so I followed the sounds to a garbage bin and lifted the lid and THERE YOU WERE!" she exclaimed.

I looked confused and said, "You found me in the GARBAGE?!"

She nodded, taking a deep drag on her cigarette and a sip of her coffee. "Yup, and you were dirty and stinky and obviously no one wanted you, so I felt sorry for you and plucked you out of the dumpster, cleaned you off and took you home."

I stared at her suspiciously, pondering her words and wondering why someone would leave a baby in a dumpster. "You're lying!" I yelled. "Nobody would do that, Mom!"

Laughing at my response, she nodded and told me the real story.

"Your dad was older than me and he had been married before," she began. "He had two older daughters but he was separated from his wife. He was blonde and blue-eyed like you are," she paused, smiling at me.

I sat there, anxious for more information. I needed to know everything so I asked, "Why isn't he here?"

"I told him I didn't want to get married, so he left. He moved to another city," she said, shrugging her shoulders. She explained how she ended up moving into an unwed mother's home when she was pregnant, where she met other girls in the same situation.

"I was going to give you up for adoption," she said, puffing on her cigarette and looking at me. I wasn't sure what adoption meant so I sat there staring at her, pretending I did and waiting for more of the story. "There was this one woman who was 30 years old who was going to do the same thing. I couldn't understand how someone her age would give her kid away. So I decided to keep you."

Give me away? What the hell, I thought. Why would you give a kid away?

"Are you glad that you did?" I asked, wide-eyed, hoping she would say yes.

"Some days," she said, laughing. I joined in the laughter, knowing she was kidding. Sort of.

"What else?" I asked. "Tell me more."

"Well, the night that you were born, I was watching The Godfather when my water broke so I called Grandma and Grandpa and asked them to bring Dairy Queen ice cream. They got to the house, and I didn't want to go to the hospital right away because the movie wasn't over, but they made me.

"So, we went and I remember jumping up and down in the hospital room, hoping you would just fall out because it hurt so damn much," she said, shaking her head at the memory. "The nurses had to calm me down and eventually you popped out!"

"Just like that?" I asked.

"Just like that," she replied. "And you were the ugliest thing I'd ever seen. But I kept you anyway."

Every once in a while, we would have conversations like that one and she would inject her insane sense of humour and say exactly what she wanted to say without really thinking about who she might offend or whether I actually understood.

"Hey Tamara," she said. "Tell Grandma what you want to be when you grow up."

"A hooker and a pill popper!" I proudly declared. I was about five or six at the time and had no idea what the hell a hooker or a pill popper was.

"DEBBIE!" my grandma yelled, unable to hide her amusement. "What the hell are you teaching her that for?"

My mom laughed and I looked around, unsure of how to act. Was it supposed to be funny? Was that what I was going to be when I grew up? Was it a bad thing? I knew if my grandma thought it was funny that it couldn't be that bad but I instinctively knew it wasn't something I should tell my teacher.

My mom going for shock value. Yes. Yes, she is making a reference to size here

Me and my mom circa 1977

She wasn't exactly a career woman, but I do remember my mom working as a waitress in a seedy bar called the Cromdale. I was about four years old when we lived in a house behind the Cromdale and my mom would go to work for the night shift, leaving me with a babysitter. One night, the babysitter left and my mom came home to a dark house with me sleeping.

She woke me up, asking where the babysitter was, but I didn't know. The next thing I knew the police were there and my mom was crying about $200 that was stolen from the house. The next night, my mom had to go to work but had no one to babysit so she just locked the door, told me not to let anyone in and went to work.

This went on for a while until we ended up getting kicked out of that place for not paying the rent or something like that. Ironically, that house was condemned and torn down after we moved.

The next place was worse but it was home for two years. She started a real job in an office, taking the bus to work and I remember watching in awe as she dressed up and walked away to catch her bus.

She was so glamorous and fancy in her skirt and heels, with her hair and makeup done. I wanted to be like her, I thought. I imagined that one day, I would dress up and catch the bus and go to an office downtown.

That job didn't last long because her new boyfriend didn't want her to get dressed up and go to work, so she went on welfare to make him happy.

He moved in and she spent her days selling Tupperware and her nights at the bar with him.

One thing she loved to do was sing and have fun. She'd sing all the time and had stacks of albums on the living room floor, stored in plastic crates. I would flip through the various records, closing my eyes when I got to Meatloaf's *Bat Out of Hell* album because I thought it was evil but loved when she cranked it up and sang along. We listened to everything from Dolly Parton to KISS (another band that traumatized me with their scary makeup), and she would sing happily along, not caring who heard her.

Her other favourite thing to do was to shock people with her filthy jokes. At seven, I didn't get her jokes but I knew they weren't things most people liked because the other adults, mostly great aunts and cousins, shook their heads and just rolled their eyes. The men, on the other hand, were amused with her twisted sense of humour. I liked that she didn't seem to care what anyone thought or how they judged her behaviour.

She just did her thing, and if you didn't like it, she would gladly tell you where to go and how to get there.

I loved my mom and thought she was so beautiful. She had this huge smile that radiated happiness and a knowing wink that made you laugh because there was so much more to what she was saying.

I don't think my mom ever looked at herself in the mirror and thought she was beautiful. She did, however, see herself as a sexpot and thought she was pretty hot, but she couldn't see deeper than that and realize just how beautiful her soul was. It's probably because no one else around her could see it either, let alone mention it to her.

During this time, we were evicted again and the house was condemned and torn down. I began to think it was normal to live in a decrepit house where you used kitchen knives to lock yourself in a room when people were fighting or that everybody had prostitutes and drug dealers hanging out in their living room on the weekends.

Time passed and we moved again. It was around this time in my life that I went overseas to live with my grandparents in Kuwait. While I was gone, my mom sent me pictures and letters, keeping me updated on life back home. Nothing seemed to change and every time I spoke with my mom, I wanted to go back to take care of her.

My grandparents stopped letting me talk to my mom because I would get so homesick that I would cry for days when she called.

Living in Kuwait was the greatest experience of my childhood. I was enrolled in a private school, took horseback riding lessons, was placed in swimming lessons at the private club we belonged to and had a maid and gardener who lived at our house.

It was the craziest thing! I went from living in houses that were condemned and torn down right after we moved out to having a maid bring me hot chocolate whenever I buzzed for her. My grandma put a stop to that as soon as she found out that I was buzzing for the maid at all hours of the night.

What can I say? I was eight years old and felt like I'd won the lottery! My grandma wouldn't put up with any pretentious behaviour and reminded me to be grateful for what I had and not treat anyone like I was better than them.

In school, I joined every club I could find that would take me and I absorbed as much of the Muslim culture as possible.

"No, Tamara, you cannot take the Islam class. You are Canadian, not Arabic," my teacher told me.

Looking around at the other students in my class, I saw that my blonde hair and blue eyes stood out in a sea of dark hair, eyes and skin; however, I was undaunted by my teacher's comment and replied, "No, but I am part Indian."

My teacher looked skeptical and said, "How so?"

I replied that my grandma was Indian and so was my mom and even my stepdad was Indian.

"Is that so?" she replied.

"It sure is," I said, my heart racing, knowing I was intentionally misleading her because I wanted to study Islam. My great-grandmother was a full-blooded, proud Cree woman and my grandmother was Métis. In 1984 where I grew up, we simply referred to ourselves as Indian so I wasn't being disrespectful of the culture. I was an eight-year-old girl who simply wanted to learn about the Islamic religion.

My teacher didn't believe me but she allowed me to start the process of taking the class with the caveat that she and the headmistress meet with my grandparents. That's when I knew the jig would be up, but I went ahead with attending the class regardless if it would have been the only one.

My grandparents were surprised to get a call from the school and shook their heads in amusement at my deception.

"Let her take the damn class," my grandfather argued. "She obviously wants to learn, so why would you deny her the opportunity?"

My grandpa was ornery, persuasive and straightforward.

My grandma, however, took a more diplomatic approach.

"We are Native American Indians," she clarified, "so she didn't technically lie to you. We respect that the class is for Islamic students only. However, shouldn't you be willing to accept a student who is eager to learn the culture?"

I sat there looking at my lap, just hoping I could, like my grandfather said, take the damn class. Eventually, the headmistress agreed to let me attend and it was the first time a Canadian student was enrolled in the course.

I faithfully attended private tutoring on Saturday mornings to catch up to the other students and was excited to learn as much as possible.

The whole experience was an awakening of my soul to the fact that there was more than one way of living.

It was then that I knew I could never follow one belief system because I found the beauty in different schools of thought. However, at eight, it wasn't so eloquently framed in my mind. It just was.

I turned nine in Kuwait and had the most extravagant birthday ever. There was cake and balloons and gifts and I got a fancy new party dress. It was by far the best birthday I'd ever had.

We travelled to Paris during spring break where my grandma and I had our hair done because, you know, when you're in Paris, you have to have your hair styled! We shopped and went to the Eiffel Tower where I melted down and pouted the entire time. About what? Who knows.

Aside from our trip to Paris, we went to London, Rome and Amsterdam. I was quickly getting used to flying in First Class and wanted to live with my grandparents forever.

My mom wouldn't let me stay with my grandparents for another year so I returned home that summer. After all of the experiences I had with my grandparents, I started to see my mom in a different light. It could have been that I was exposed to a different way of living or that I was seeing how drastically my mom had changed but I was beginning to get angry with the way my mom was living her life.

Throwing a pouty fit on the Eiffel Tower during Spring Break - 1985

Celebrating my ninth
birthday with my
grandparents in Kuwait

LESSONS I HAD TO LEARN

Over the next couple of years, I watched my mom transition from a vivacious, charismatic woman into a bitter, broken soul, and it was all due to one relationship that lasted about 20 years. Each moment she stayed with him – every beating, every glare, every accusation and every vile word that spewed from his mouth – chipped away at her confidence. I saw her deteriorate from the young mom I loved so much to a woman I couldn't stand to be around.

"Keep this knife in the door like this and don't open it unless I tell you to." She said, sliding a large kitchen knife between the door and the door frame as a lock. Her mascara was messy from crying and her lipstick was smeared. I could smell cigarettes and booze mixed with her perfume as she grabbed my shoulders, shaking me.

"Tamara! Do you understand?! I'm not fucking around here!"

"Yes," I stammered, my heart pounding.

It was the middle of the night and I had heard them come home; he was screaming at her and she was begging him to stop. Chairs were being knocked down, dishes that had been left on the counter were being smashed, and the sound of his fist connecting with her head was unmistakable. I'd heard it all a hundred times before but it never got easier.

She left me in the bedroom and returned to the fight. Anytime the police were called, things were worse the next time they got drunk and eventually, she stopped calling the cops. It didn't matter anyway. She'd tell them she was sorry for bothering them, that it was a mistake, that she tripped and that it wasn't his fault. It was never his fault. She instigated it, she talked back, and she pushed him too far.

Every once in a while, she decided enough was enough and she went to a shelter. She'd cry and tell the worker how scared she was and how she feared for her life and they'd give us a bed to stay for the night. Within a couple of days, he'd sweet talk her into coming back. He'd never do it again, it was the alcohol, and she should know better than to use that smart mouth for something other than what it was made for.

This wasn't the first time a guy treated her like this but he was the one who stuck around the longest. He'd been around long enough that I decided to call him dad.

She began to take her anger out on everyone around her, as many domestic abuse victims tend to do. She lashed out both physically and verbally, using the same words that were used to strip away the layers of her dignity, projecting every ounce of her anger onto me. She hardened into someone I couldn't even recognize, and I began to hate her.

When I was 11 years old, he decided to teach me a few things about being a grownup.

It would start with an "accidental" touch here and there, masked as fatherly affection, and escalated to aggressive physical and sexual abuse.

The details don't matter; all of it was enough to scar me for the rest of my life.

I was suddenly thrust into living a double life where I went to school as a happy, fairly social and above average Grade 6 student to going home and being terrified of pissing him off for fear of the consequences.

If I talked back, he wouldn't hesitate to backhand me.

If I pushed it, he would choke me until I almost lost consciousness.

If I looked at him the wrong way, he would pull off his belt and pull down my pants, taking pleasure in making me count how many times he would hit me. It was sadistic and humiliating and he loved every minute of it.

The sexual abuse was masked as this loving "father-daughter" relationship. We were "so close" that it was understandable why he was so cuddly and affectionate. When my mom wasn't around, the affection went beyond touching and fondling.

As bad as things got and as plentiful as the opportunities were, I never got into drugs or rebelled because I seriously was afraid of what would happen if he found out. If I didn't back down from his intimidation tactics, the violence could get pretty nasty.

I learned to shut my mouth when I thought I had pushed too far, but his temper was unpredictable.

It wasn't just him, either. My mom became violent and emotionally abusive. She changed from the mom who was fun-loving and playful to an angry, bitter person who lashed out because of the violence she was suffering at his hands. I know that now, but when I was 12, I was confused and hated her, missing the mom I knew and adored.

In the summer before I went into Grade 9, we had moved for the umpteenth time and the abuse got worse. I went to school one day with a scarf wrapped around my neck as an accessory to my outfit. One of the boys at school thought it would be funny to pull it off and run away with it but when he did he uncovered the hickey I was trying to cover up.

My language arts teacher, the one teacher I wanted to impress the most because her sister a was journalist and I wanted to be a writer of some sort, looked at me with disappointment and disgust, shaking her head saying, "I didn't know you were one of 'those' girls."

I was ashamed and wanted to cry but instead I just shrugged.

Like many kids who suffer at the hands of an abuser, I didn't tell anybody about what was happening to me. I was worried about the consequences, certain that no one would help me, terrified that no one would believe me and afraid of losing my "family."

We moved again the summer before I went to high school and things took a turn for the worst. Looking back, I'm sure my mom was bipolar. She went from extreme highs to extreme lows and I was the focus of her rage.

"You stupid fucking bitch!" she yelled.

"Takes one to know one," I replied, glaring back at her. I wasn't about to break down and cry or show any sort of weakness in front of her. I wasn't weak like her.

SMACK!

"Get the fuck out of my house and don't come back! Go fucking be a whore and make some money, you filthy cunt. You are never going to be anything but a whore."

I couldn't help myself. I could feel myself start to break. "Where am I supposed to go?" I was terrified to leave and didn't want to stay but I had no idea what the hell to do.

"I don't fucking care where you go, just get the fuck out!" And with that, she whipped a fork at me that landed firmly in my thigh.

I looked up at her in horror with this stupid fork sticking out of my leg and yelled, "What the fuck kind of mother ARE you?!"

I yanked it out and ran out the door, sitting on the outside steps and holding my head in my hands, sobbing. I hated her. I hated everything about her and wished I could just run away and break free from my life. Sitting there, I looked at the four holes in my thigh where the fork had pierced my flesh, thinking how messed up my life was.

She wasn't the mom I remembered; years of alcohol, drugs, physical and emotional abuse stole her away from me but she chose that life and chose to stay in the relationship that got her there.

All I knew was that I had to get out of that house and make it out in one piece.

Eventually I did, but it wasn't in one piece.

Every once in a while my mom would offer glimpses of her former self, often through unexpected shows of affection or by whisking me off to bingo with her instead of leaving me at home with him. The best surprise was for my 15th birthday when she bought tickets to an elegant gala dinner featuring Edmonton Oilers hottie Craig Simpson. The tickets cost $50 each, which was a LOT of money for her because welfare didn't allow for luxuries like that, so I was grateful and thrilled that she would invest her money into something so indulgent just for me. I had the biggest crush on Craig Simpson and aspirations of becoming a sports writer, so this gala dinner was my first taste of my career ambitions.

It was a fancy dinner and a crowd neither my mom nor I were used to being around. Needless to say we were both out of our comfort zones, and I was far too shy to ask Craig for a picture but that was the great thing about my mom; the word "shy" wasn't in her vocabulary. She tugged on Craig's sleeve and asked if he would pose for a picture with me. He did, even putting his arm around me and I had this ridiculously goofy fangirl smile.

I left that night feeling on top of the world and thinking my life really could be better than it was. I was going to be a sportswriter, I thought, and I would get to mingle with celebrities and interview people and live in a highrise apartment and dress in fancy clothes! My aspirations exploded into a thousand stars that night and I believed in the possibility of success and happiness for myself.

The next morning, I got on the bus to go to school, eyes half closed with fatigue and accidentally kicked the crutches of a severely disabled kid who was sitting in the front seat. I was horrified, humiliated at my stupidity and had no idea what to do. I crouched in the corner of a bus seat, hiding in shame and really did want to die, I felt so bad.

The thing is, I didn't do what I knew I should have done. I didn't pick up the crutches; I just hid on the bus seat. Another passenger picked them up and berated me for being so ignorant.

In my mind, I told myself I deserved to be punished. Happiness, I began to understand, could never be experienced without incredible suffering.

That night, I got home and endured one of the worst beatings I had ever taken from my stepdad. His excuse was that he had found a phone number from a boy and if I was going to act like a slut, I deserved to be treated like one.

I begged, tried to reason with him, fought back and eventually submitted to the punishment knowing that, just like the other times, it wouldn't last forever. He left my room but not without threatening that if I ever told anyone, the next time would be worse.

I was covered head to toe in bruises from where he kicked me with his steel-toed boots. My hair was a tangled mess and I couldn't stop shaking. I looked in my mirror and broke down, sobbing uncontrollably at my reflection.

I pictured myself going upstairs and taking a kitchen knife, stabbing him repeatedly until I felt no more pain. I saw myself killing him and in that same moment, I saw my future.

"You'll end up in jail, your family will be ruined and you will never have a life," I told myself.

The only thing that stopped me from going upstairs was the idea of not having a future. Instead, I slumped onto the floor and continued to cry, begging silently for anyone to help me.

No help ever came. I told myself I deserved the beating because of what happened on the bus. It was my fault and karma was paying me back for being so thoughtless.

"If you can just finish high school, you'll be able to leave. Just tough it out, Tamara," I mumbled to myself. "Take the beatings, take the pain, take it all, just focus. In a couple of years this will be nothing but a bad memory."

"Don't take life so seriously. You'll never get out of it alive."

I had that saying on a poster hanging in my room. I liked it because, to me, it meant that no matter what happened in life the end result was the same for everyone, so you might as well have a GREAT time while you're here. My stepdad saw it one night in a drunken rage and was looking for reasons to pick a fight so he pointed at it and demanded to know if I planned on killing myself or him.

Yeah, I thought. I'd kill you in a heartbeat if I didn't have to risk the rest of my life paying for it, you dumb fuck.

"No, of course not," I replied, cowering as he raised his hand. The

words fell out of my mouth, not making any sense as he glared at me, enraged. I braced myself for what was to come and just turtled instead of fighting back when he hit me.

My bedroom was in the basement of the last house I would ever live in with my mom. It had dingy, cold cement floors and only a thin, hollow door with a wood veneer surface separating me from the violent outbursts that would often occur. Some nights, on that dank and dirty floor, I would huddle under a blanket that I had draped over a floor heater just to keep warm. Looking back, it's a miracle I didn't set myself on fire but I had no other way to stay warm and no idea of the possibility my blanket igniting. It was simply something I did to survive. When my grandma found out what I was doing, she made me a quilt to stay warm.

"Here, if this doesn't keep you warm, you'll have to find a boyfriend," she laughed.

I managed to convince myself that I just had to make it through the next couple of years. One day, in the middle of all of the craziness, I was given a perfectly wrapped gift from the universe in the form of another move. This time, it would take us to another town where I would be isolated and completely vulnerable to him. But this time, I refused to go. I was just starting my Grade 12 year and only 16 years old so I argued that I needed to finish high school where I had started. I had a part-time job, I was on the volleyball team, I was the editor of the yearbook and there was no way in hell I was going to let him win this time.

For some reason, both he and my mom agreed to let me stay and finish school.

The next seven months stretched out before me and I finally tasted the freedom I had always craved. My mom continued her downward spiral but I no longer cared.

All I cared about was saving myself.

When grad came around, I was posing for pictures with my high school crush when my stepdad came over and pulled me aside for a photo, putting his arm around me like the doting dad he was.

Through his creepy grin, he whispered, "So how long has this been going on?"

I smiled for the camera and replied, "If you ruin this for me, I will never forgive you."

That night, in a drunken rage, he picked me up and threw me across the room, calling me a slut. "You think you're free now?" he yelled. "You think you're going to get away?"

My mom just stood there, not saying a word. He backhanded me across the face, yanking a fistful of my hair and forcing me to look at him. Hate filled his eyes as he wrapped his hands around my throat and squeezed. It wasn't the first time but I knew it would be the last time. Finally, my mom yelled at him to stop. He shook me and threw me to the floor, turning around and slapping her for saying something.

I picked myself up, coughing, and glared at him.

"You can't do a fucking thing to me anymore, you pervert! I'm never going to let you touch me again!"

And with that, I grabbed my shoes and ran out the door. I slept in the park that night, not caring about anything. I had no money, nowhere to go and no idea what the hell I was going to do. That was the first day of my summer as a free person and I was homeless. I was 17 and spent a lot of nights sleeping in the park but some nights I couch-surfed. I had a part-time job in a corner grocery store for 15 hours a week making $5 an hour and no idea how to get my life on track.

The one time I did go to see my mom, I told her about the abuse I had suffered all those years.

She sat there, looking dumbfounded and shook her head in disbelief.

"No," she said, puffing on her cigarette. "I would have known."

"You were so fucking absent, when would you have noticed," I yelled, frustrated with her constant victim mentality.

"No, you two were so close," she said, tearing up. "You were always playful and you liked it."

"Yeah, I loved being touched by that fucking pervert, MOM! Why are you still with him? Why do you let him push you around and hit you and control every fucking thing?!"

She had no words and her silence was her answer. She chose him. Simple as that.

After that conversation, I spent less and less time with my mom.

For most of my teenage years, she drowned her pain in alcohol and bingo, two things that seemed to offer an escape from her miserable world and the choices she had made.

For me, it was time to take control of my future and start thinking about how I was going to make those big dreams I had of becoming a sports writer a reality.

Me and former Edmonton Oilers star
Craig Simpson. I was 15 and
convinced I was going to marry him

FROM DARKNESS

I had made it through the worst and was finally able to start my life. It didn't matter that I had nowhere to live and no idea how to become a sports writer. I was on my own and no one could ever hurt me again.

Life could only get better, right?

Wrong.

A couple of weeks after that final confrontation with my stepdad, I found out that my grandmother had been diagnosed with lung cancer.

I was so wrapped up in my own problems that I didn't see the gravity of the situation. The summer dragged on and I never knew where I would end up from day to day. Sometimes I would stay with friends masked as a "sleepover" and other times I would crash at a wayward relative's place. I rarely stayed with them unless the alternative meant sleeping outside and sometimes the neighbourhood park was the better alternative.

When my grandma found out what I was doing, she was livid. She was determined to find a safe place for me to live, far away from the inner city and preferably with someone who was a responsible adult. She was also determined to do this before she went back to Kuwait to be with my grandpa. By some stroke of luck, she met a sweet, little old lady named Tilly who was volunteering at a second-hand shop that my grandma visited.

"I want you on your best behaviour," warned my grandma. "Don't you be crass or say anything to screw this up."

I rolled my eyes but was secretly excited at the thought of living in a basement suite of my own in a neighbourhood where rich people lived. I mean, Edmonton Oilers' owner Peter Pocklington's MANSION was in that neighbourhood! I also believed it was a sign that I could really become a sports writer who covered the Oilers. Obviously, some great power was putting me on that path if I was practically going to be Pocklington's neighbour!

Once I was settled, my grandma went back to Kuwait happily knowing that I was no longer homeless.

Let me tell you a little bit about my grandmother. She was barely over five feet tall, which meant I towered over her by five inches, but her personality made her six-foot-eight.

She was 38 when I was born, and carried herself with the poise and sophistication of no one else I had ever met. However, she wasn't averse to getting her hands dirty and working hard to make ends meet.

She took pride in having put herself through school to become a hairdresser and she believed that no one was above cleaning a toilet. In fact, she believed doing so would keep you humble and she constantly reminded me not to think I was better than anyone else.

My grandma would regale me with tales of wild days spent with my grandfather when they were younger. She was no angel and she was OK with that because she didn't hold onto the guilt or shame other people might have held her to.

I often wondered how she could possibly have raised my mom, who was nothing like my grandma. My mom made stupid choices and constantly turtled into the victim mentality whereas my grandma wouldn't even put up with my grandfather telling her what to make for supper.

My only childhood memories that provide comfort are the ones that include my grandparents. My grandma would tuck me into bed, a kerosene lamp softly glowing on the bedside table, and would give me a small plate of fruit and cookies and tell me sweet stories about Cookie Monster going to visit his grandma.

My grandma also told me about angels and how they protected you no matter how bad things seemed. She said they were always with you even though you couldn't see them. I would close my eyes and sleep in peace knowing nothing bad would happen to me when I was there.

My grandpa and I would watch hockey together and I'm sure I became an Oilers fan to piss him off because he was so dedicated to his Calgary Flames.

Occasionally, when things were bad at home, I would sneak a phone call to my grandma and whisper, "Grandma, come get me!" My grandpa would pick me up and take me to their place despite the rage and threats my mom would unleash at his expense.

My grandmother looked after me over the years and protected me when she could. She was tough, fearless and one of the few people I respected enough to not talk back to.

She wasn't going to let a little thing like lung cancer get in her way of living life.

Having a stable address meant I could also apply for other jobs. I went back to school for a second year of Grade 12, mainly because I needed something to do with my life and still believed I could make this dream I had of becoming a sports writer come true.

My grandparents' wedding circa 1982

I had no idea how to apply for college and now that my grandma was halfway around the world, no one to lean on for guidance or advice.

Instead of making the most of the opportunity to go back to school and live in a stable environment, I fucked it up by skipping classes and only staying to play volleyball. Tilley became very unhappy with my coming and going all the time, and less than two months after moving in, told me I couldn't live with her anymore. She wanted someone who would keep her company but I wasn't interested in that so I packed up my two black garbage bags full of stuff and had my mom pick me up.

Once again, I had no idea what I was going to do.

I'd started dating my high school crush right after I'd left home after the confrontation, and his dad took pity on me, saying I could stay at their house until I figured out what I was going to do. A week turned into a month and the next thing you know, six months went by and I was still there. It wasn't perfect but at least I wasn't homeless again or, worse, living with my mom.

I left high school after the first half of the year was over, still insisting to myself that I really would be up on that catwalk above the Oilers' rink, covering the team and living the life I wanted.

Every once in a while, when I knew my stepdad wouldn't be around, I would visit my mom, strangely enough finding comfort in being around her and being in the old neighbourhood. I missed my mom. Not the mom she was when I was in my early teens but the mom whose smile could change the dynamic in a room, the mom who laughed and sang out loud when she was happy. I missed my mom, simple as that.

In the spring of '93, my grandma came back to Edmonton because her condition was getting worse. She found a 300-square-foot studio apartment and said we could share it so that she didn't have to be alone. Even though I didn't have my licence, I would drive her to her radiation appointments and take care of her as best as I could, which really wasn't that great since I could barely figure out how to take care of myself.

"Hey, Grandma, that old guy is giving you the eye," I whispered across the table as we sat in a bingo hall, and laughed at her reaction.

She looked around, beaming, and when she caught his eye, she turned back and slapped my hand with her bingo marker.

"GRANDMA!!" I whispered loudly, not wanting to disturb the other bingo players. "What the hell, woman!?"

She laughed at me and said, "He's not my type. He's old."

I shook my head, giggling at the thought of my grandma flirting with someone other than my grandpa. It made me happy knowing that she loved life so much. Everywhere we went, people were drawn to her, whether it was her warmth and generosity or her down-to-earth sensibility. She seemed to know everything.

The old Bonanza seller walked past our table again, whistling "That's Amore" and winked at my grandma. I started singing loudly enough that my grandma could hear and we both laughed.

"When the moon hits your eye like a big piece of pie that's Amoraaaaaaaaay!" I sang to my grandma, laughing at her as she gave me a dirty look.

"It's pizza pie not piece of pie," she corrected.

"Why the hell would you get hit in the eye with a pizza?" I replied, laughing. "Pizzas aren't pies! They're pizzas. It's piece of pie ... When the moon hits your eye like a big PIECE OF PIE that's amoraaaaaaaay!"

We both started to laugh hysterically, tears streaming down our faces while people shushed us to be quiet.

"Tamara," my grandma said, motioning for me to lean across the table, "I have to tell you something."

I did and she put me in a headlock rubbing her bingo dabber all over my face.

"GRANDMA!" I squealed, pulling back. "WHAT THE DAMN HELL!?"

We both laughed so hard that we missed the entire calling of that game.

My grandma decided to move back to the acreage she and my grandpa bought a few years back. They had rented it out but she wanted to get out of the city and back to nature, where she was the happiest.

Before she moved, my mom came over to visit us in the little apartment. I was tired and really didn't want to talk to my mom so I closed the divider from the living room and had a nap. I was deep in dreamland when I heard someone knocking at the door.

I got up and went to answer it. It was my grandma's sister who had passed away the year before from cancer.

She stood there, her hair in a beehive hairdo and way too much blue eye shadow but I knew it was her.

"Um. What are you doing here?" I asked, not sure if I was awake or asleep.

"Tell your grandma that it's OK," she said.

"What? What the hell does that mean?!"

"Tell her everything will be OK. It's beautiful here."

I started to panic, my heart heavy with grief and wondered what the hell a dead relative was doing at my door. I was confused and weirded out and sat up in bed, drenched in sweat. I could hear my mom and grandma chatting away on the other side of the divider. Shaking my head and wiping my eyes, I got up and pulled the divider open. They both looked up at me and stopped their conversation.

"What's wrong, my girl?" my mom asked.

"You look whiter than usual," my grandma said, chuckling. "Bad dream?"

I looked at them both and said, "I had a dream about Aunty Carol. It was so weird. She had this beehive hairdo and bad makeup and she said to tell you it was OK."

My grandma went still and held her breath. The colour drained from her face and she said, "What did you say?"

"She told me to tell you that it's OK," I replied. "Whatever the hell that means. She said it's beautiful and that it's OK."

I was still trying to rationalize how a dream could feel so real and wanted to dismiss it.

"That wasn't a dream, Tamara," she said. The look of concern on my mom's face was enough to tell me something bigger than I understood had happened.

"A few years ago, Carol and I were having coffee late one night and we made a deal that whoever died first had to come back and tell the other one what it was like."

I felt like someone punched me in the stomach. "What?"

"She came to you. That wasn't a dream," my grandma replied. "She came to you to give me a message. You have a gift."

"You're crazy. That isn't a thing. Dead people don't come back and talk to you!"

"It runs in the family, Tamara. You're not the only one who is in touch with the other side."

No way, I thought. That was a dream. No fucking way were dead relatives coming to visit me. I wouldn't have it. My grandma was clearly losing her shit.

"Sure, whatever," I replied, unable to shake the feeling of how real that dream was.

Dream or not, I wasn't about to start talking to spirits or any other voodoo crazy crap like that so I dismissed the whole situation.

About a month later, my grandma ended up in the hospital and my grandpa came back to Canada to take care of her. He decided to have her released from the hospital so that they could be at home. She wasn't that sick, I thought, if she was going home. I planned on going to see her but never got around to it.

On July 20, 1993, the night before my grandpa was supposed to return to Kuwait, she died in his arms.

Everything happened so quickly, and I felt like my world was spinning out of control. I had no idea how to deal with losing my grandma. She was the one person who guided me, who gave me a sense of direction, who believed in me and who I actually listened to. Her death meant I was completely alone. I couldn't count on my mom to be a mom, and my grandfather was going back to work overseas.

I looked around at the funeral, at relatives I wanted nothing to do with and people I had no respect for, and finally understood what I had lost.

"Tamara, how are you doing?" someone asked, pulling me into a hug. I completely broke down and started sobbing uncontrollably.

"I don't know what I'm going to do," I cried as my entire body shook with grief. It lasted for about a minute before I realized I had let my guard down. I pulled away and choked back the tears.

Stop it, I told myself. Get your shit together. Don't let anyone see you break down, ever again! I took deep breaths and walked away. I don't even remember saying goodbye to my grandfather or how I got home. The next few months passed and I did my best to forget. It was simply one more thing to go through, I thought. People left. People died. People hurt you. And no one seemed to give a fuck about how I was coping or what I was going to do with my life.

Except my grandfather.

We hadn't spent any time together since the year I had lived in Kuwait with my grandparents, but after my grandma died, he would call me to see how I was doing and reminisce about her.

"What do you plan on doing with your life?" he asked.

"I don't know," I replied. "I want to be a sports writer."
"So? Go do it."

It was simple for him. If you wanted to do something, you did it. You didn't sit around and feel sorry for yourself or come up with a thousand reasons why you couldn't do something. Instead, you got off your ass and made your life happen. He had some idea about what I had been through but he never asked me about it. Instead, he'd force me to look ahead and figure out how to make something out of myself.

"You can't live in the past," he reminded me. "Get over it. Your mom made mistakes, you've made mistakes and life goes on. If you don't want to do anything with your life, then keep doing what you're doing because you will never get anywhere in life. But your grandma wouldn't want that, so get your head out of your ass and smarten up!"

If anyone else had said that to me, I would have told them to fuck off before slamming the phone down. But it was my grandpa and he was the only person I had ever known to work for what he wanted and to be successful in a career. And now that my grandma was gone, he was the only person I truly respected. I was ready to believe in myself enough to chase that dream.

When I made the decision to apply to a journalism program, it was as though every red light had turned green and everything was starting to work out in my favour.

"How do I know that you're not going to be one of those kids who gets in then wastes my time by not taking this seriously?"

I looked at the professor during my interview and said, "Because I'm not going to end up like everyone else in my family. You don't know me. You don't know what I've been through to get here. I'll be the first person in my entire family EVER to go to college whether it's here or whether I have to wait another year. Either way, I'm going.

"The only thing I've ever wanted to be was a sports writer and I know I can do it, but I also know I need to work to get it. I am determined to make that happen and I'll do whatever it takes to make it happen. I can't give up on this because it's the only thing I have left."

Taking a deep breath, I looked at him, determined not to show how truly terrified I was at the thought of not getting in.

"OK," he said.

"OK, what?" I replied. "Does that mean I'm getting in?"
He looked up from my application and grinned. "Between you and me, you're in. I can't say it officially but, yeah, you're in."

Holy shit, holy shit, HOLY SHIT, I thought to myself, mentally cheering and dancing.

"I won't let you down," I said, standing up to shake his hand. If it was possible to die from happiness, I would have dropped dead right there.

Being accepted into the diploma program at Mount Royal College (now University) in Calgary meant I had to leave my life in Edmonton behind. The challenge for me was that I wasn't quite ready to leave my mom behind and move on with my life.

I frequently made trips back to Edmonton to see her, finding some comfort being in the old neighbourhood and feeling like I needed to be there to remember where I came from. If I wanted to, I could have started a new life without any ties to my past but I couldn't bring myself to do it.

College was the first realization that something was wrong with me. I couldn't figure out how to act around people who seemed to have such perfect lives. Memories of the sexual abuse started to take over my waking consciousness, and in order to drown them out, I spent far too much time at nightclubs and was ready to fight anyone anytime I felt threatened.

The rage I had kept eating away at me and I couldn't figure out why. I forced myself to focus on fulfilling this dream of becoming a sports writer by immersing myself into working on the school paper and looking for any way to get into the industry. I couldn't maintain any friendships because I was so emotionally volatile.

Anytime I went out, I would either end up in a fight or crying over some stupid guy. It was really pathetic and no wonder I couldn't maintain any relationships. I wouldn't have wanted to be friends with me.

I knew that if I spent too much time with the kids in my class that they would see right past the facade I had built and realize what a fraud I really was. I didn't belong there with these students whose families seemed perfect and who never had to survive anything. The more I thought about it, the more lost I felt. I started skipping classes and going back to Edmonton to see my mom.

"So drop out," she suggested. "Get a job. Live here. Don't worry about it."

"Yeah, I should probably find a guy who'll beat me up and I can live on welfare, too," I sneered.

All I needed was to end up like my mom and I knew that if I gave up, I might. I couldn't let that happen.

At the beginning of my second semester, the NHL lockout ended and, since I was a sports writer for the college paper, I decided to see if I could swing an interview with some of the players who were returning to the ice.

It was a dream come true. The Edmonton Oilers were set to play the Calgary Flames and, as someone who grew up watching the Battle of Alberta rivalry, the idea of interviewing those players was another step towards building my career.

I walked down to the dressing room after practice and stood outside of the locker room door, glancing inside and hoping for a glimpse of something I shouldn't see. My first interview was with Theo Fleury and I managed to piss him off by asking a stupid question.

It was the arrogance of youth and a complete lack of professionalism on my part. I didn't care, though. At the time, it felt like I had won the career lottery by scoring interviews no one else at the school paper was able to.

When I was focused on my goals, it was easier to suppress everything else: I was away from my mom, I didn't have to think about the abuse and I had no reason to rage out on anyone because I had to focus completely on my goal.

Before the end of my second semester, I took a leap of faith and sent an email to the *Edmonton Journal* sports desk and boldly asked to be an intern for the summer.

For once, the universe seemed to take pity on me, and within a week, I had secured a spot and was set to work in the same room as my journalism idols, Cam Cole and Jim Matheson. I couldn't believe my luck and was determined not to screw it up.

My only goal was to impress the editor so much that he would hire me after the internship.

"What are you working on?" he asked.

"Well, I wrote a column, kind of a sarcastic piece but more my writing style than the stuff I've been doing so far," I replied. "It's just for fun, nothing serious." I was completely intimidated but didn't want to let the editor in on my insecurities so I just sat there, awkward and unsure of myself.

He walked behind the desk and read over my shoulder as I silently cringed, expecting him to criticize my work. Instead, he laughed a couple of times and some of the other reporters looked over.

To my complete surprise, he put his hand on my shoulder and said, "Good job!"

I beamed, some of my confidence returning, and stood up. "Thank you!"

"Print it off and let the other guys read it."

Without thinking twice, I did and offered it up to the other writers.

Later that day, I was chatting with the assistant editor when Jim Matheson walked over to ask him a question. I looked down, not wanting to make eye contact, but he turned to me and said, "I read that column you wrote."

Glancing up, I simply stared at him in silence, afraid to say something stupid.

"You're a better writer than I was at your age," he said, smiling before turning to talk to the editor.

I just about died right then and there. Holy shit! Jim Matheson, Hockey Hall of Fame writer and overall icon in the sports writing world, told me I was a better writer than he was at my age! That was it! I knew then and there my dreams weren't some unattainable mess in my mind; I could actually live the life I wanted to!

"Tamara, we want you to spend a day at an Eskimos day camp for women. You can write about what it's like to hit the field and learn some basics about the game."

Hell yeah, I thought. I can do this! I tucked away that nugget of confidence from Jim and pushed forward, determined to skyrocket to the life I wanted. I was going to write a column that would endear me to the editor, secure a spot on the sports desk, live in a condo in Edmonton and make enough money to never worry about anything ever again!

But when I got to the camp, I froze. I couldn't bring myself to interview anyone or talk to the coaches or even participate in the camp. Instead, I sat on the sidelines and watched everyone else participate, have fun and interact with the coaches and a couple of members of the Eskimos. I went back to the sports desk, slumped into my chair and stared at a blank screen. Minutes ticked by and turned into hours before I finally picked up the phone and called the editor.

"I can't do this," I said. "I don't know where to start."

"Just write what you can and we'll run what you have. It's OK. No one expects an award-winning piece. Keep it light, have fun with it and remember that it is supposed to be from your perspective.

"You can do this," he encouraged. "We've seen your writing and you have the skills. Start writing and see what happens."

I took a deep breath and hung up the phone. Tears started to fall on my keyboard before I realized I was crying and I put my head in my hands and sat there, wishing I could do it over again. I felt defeated, wondering if I'd ever truly make it out of the inner city. No matter where I physically was, in my head I would always be stuck in that other life.

The copy editors kept looking over at me, wondering where the column was and, although I knew it was shit when I turned it in, I sent it over and walked out of the building, knowing I wouldn't be getting a job there.

I went back to college for what would be my final semester. I had skipped enough 8 a.m. History of Journalism classes to put me on my prof's radar and by the end of the third semester, my grades had plummeted.

"If you weren't so concerned with partying and whatever other extracurricular activities you were into, you might still have a spot in this program," my prof told me. "You know, Tamara, I believed in you. You could actually be one of the few who really make it."

I knew he was pissed off that I wasn't taking school seriously but I wasn't about to let him know how devastated I was at being kicked out. It was my own fault. I had been so torn by my demons and need to cling to life in the inner city that I wasn't able to let it go and live the life I really wanted.

"Whatever. I'm confident that I will get a job in the industry."

"Confidence doesn't mean you're any good," he said before walking away.

If I could have, I would have dug a hole to crawl into and die because that didn't sting AT ALL. Instead, I had to go home and call my grandfather to tell him the news.

He was rightfully enraged and yelled at me over the phone, his disappointment stinging more than anything else. My only saving grace was that he was thousands of miles overseas and couldn't actually yell at me in person because I don't know if I could have handled seeing how heartbroken he was.

Once again, I was on a path with no idea where the hell it would lead, no light at the end of the tunnel and no clue as to how I was going to support myself.

Leaving Edmonton to go to college in Calgary, August, 1995

My very first NHL interview was with Calgary Flames star Theo Fleury

46

TO LIGHT

I had royally fucked up.

I was now out of college with no official journalism diploma and unsure of how to create my future. Obviously, the easy path was no longer an option: get a journalism diploma and get a job, easy-peasy. Instead, I figured I would charm my way into my chosen field using my obviously brilliant writing skills and insane knowledge of the NHL. No delusions of grandeur there *insert eye roll emoji here*.

As disappointed as my grandfather was in me, I refused to give up on myself. I moved back to Edmonton and took a retail job for $5.25 an hour but hit up every free rag in the city for freelancing gigs. I found a new sports magazine that had just launched, called *Sports Scene*, and walked in with my portfolio, insisting I was the missing piece to their editorial calendar.

"Want a beer?" the managing partner asked.

I knew the game.

I knew that if I wanted to break into the sports industry that I had to be one of the guys.

"Sure."

We sat there and I told them about how I was going to be a sports writer for a daily newspaper but that I needed some experience. I told them about my internship at the *Edmonton Journal* and how I scored an NHL press pass when I was in college and did a couple of interviews. I didn't tell them I was kicked out of college because, well, they didn't need to know that part. I flipped through their sports magazine and showed them where they could improve and how I could help them.

It worked and I took the first step on my new path to becoming a sports writer. I was pretty pleased with myself and decided that maybe, just maybe, the universe was on my side.

My grandfather eventually got over my stupid mistake and I repaired the fractured pieces of our relationship by proving to him that I would not give up on my career. I would send him columns and articles I was writing for *Sports Scene* and he would try to convince me that the Calgary Flames were superior to the Edmonton Oilers.

It was a back and forth, love-hate argument that bonded us and it was my favourite topic of conversation with him.

Life might not have been perfect but I was still taking steps towards making my dream come true. I found an adorable basement suite away from the inner city, owned by an Italian couple who became a second family to me. It was the first place I lived where I ever felt safe enough to sleep.

After years of a revolving door of one-night stands, I ended up meeting a guy who lived in Toronto. We talked on the phone every night for about a month, and the conversations became much more than casual chit-chat.

"Maybe you could move here and get a writing job," he suggested. "It would make things easier for us to be together."

The thought of leaving Edmonton again terrified me. I wasn't ready for that but I also knew I wanted something more in my life; I wanted a relationship.

I let myself believe that I could actually find someone to love and be happy. Maybe it was possible, I thought. Maybe I was supposed to go to Toronto and work there. The more we talked, the more I toyed with the idea of leaving. The day before my 22nd birthday, he called to tell me there was a package on its way for me. I couldn't remember the last time anyone bought me a birthday gift and it was the first time it was a from a guy I had feelings for.

When the package arrived, I ripped open the box to find a black and white striped tiger that was plush and cuddly and adorable. I opened the envelop and looked at the card.

"Happy birthday, Tamara. Love, Keon"

My heart flooded with that warm feeling you get when you know you're falling in love. I called him and we talked more about the idea of me moving to Toronto.

"I was standing outside of Eaton Centre looking at a dress and imagining you in it," he said.

I smiled, envisioning him standing there and started to picture myself there with him. I told him about my birthday plans and, before hanging up the phone, promised to call him in a couple of days.

Traditionally, I spent my birthday at a nightclub with a girlfriend and although we went to a club, I wasn't in the mood to party. All I wanted to do was get home and spend the night talking to Keon.

My girlfriend crashed at my place and we sat up most of

the night talking so I never did call him. The next day, I drove her to work and finally told her about Keon. As I did, I looked up and saw a gloriously vibrant sundog and had an overwhelming urge to call him. I stopped talking and listened to the radio as Toni Braxton sang the hauntingly beautiful lyrics of *Unbreak My Heart*.

My mood shifted from one of goopy, girly romantic to concern, and I couldn't figure out why. After dropping her off, I went back home and called him.

No answer. I tried to shake the feeling but it wouldn't go away and the more time that passed, the more I needed to talk to him.

I called again the next day and a woman's voice answered.

"Hello?"

"Um, hi. Can I speak to Keon, please?"

"Who is this?"

"It's Tamara," I replied, wondering who the hell was answering his phone.

"Are you the girl in the picture?" she asked.

"I think so. If it's the blonde in the black outfit. Who is this?"

"Keon died," she simply said. *"I'm his mom."*

I sat there in shock, wondering why the hell she would say something like that to me. Was she one of those protective moms who screened her son's girlfriends?

"I don't ..." my voice trailed off and I couldn't breathe.

"I can't talk to you right now." she yelled, handing off the phone to someone else. "Tell her what happened."

I listened as a young girl told me that Keon had died the day before. He had choked to death during an epileptic seizure. The funeral would be in a couple of days, and if I could come, I was more than welcome.

I don't remember hanging up the phone or what happened the rest of the day. I sat there in shock and disbelief, wondering how it was possible to lose someone again. I was desperate to get to the funeral, needing to see if it was real or some magnificent hoax. Maybe he decided he didn't want to be with me but couldn't tell me so instead he was faking his death. Maybe his mom intercepted a phone call because she didn't want me to be with her son. Maybe I was going to be alone forever because I didn't deserve to be happy.

The universe didn't want me at that funeral. The Edmonton Eskimos were playing in the Grey Cup final in Toronto the same day he was going to be buried. There were no flights available and even if there were, I had no money to get there.

"Mom, I don't know what to do," I said. "What do I do?"

I could see the concern on her face and she said, "I don't know, my girl."

I kept in touch with Keon's mom, mostly to have someone to talk to. She listened to me and understood what I was going through, often telling me stories about him and reminding me that he was always with us. I don't know if I helped her as much as she helped me but I was grateful for her support.

I wrestled with my personal demons, even though I didn't think there was anything wrong with me, and I floundered through the next few months, spending my time at nightclubs and making a lot of bad decisions.

During the days, I would focus on doing anything I could to turn my vision of becoming a sports writer a reality; at night I would desperately try to escape my demons and drown the memories that would flood my consciousness when it was too dark and too quiet.

Sitting in the waiting room, I filled out the questionnaire and looked around and wondered what was really wrong with me. I wasn't coughing, I wasn't aching anywhere; physically I felt fine but I knew I wasn't OK.

"The doctor will see you now," the nurse said, guiding me into a patient room. I sat there, unsure of myself, and stared at the images on the wall of a human heart and other basic anatomy. I looked at the jar filled with cotton balls and tongue depressors.

I glanced over at the blood pressure machine and sighed. I wasn't sick, I thought, and got up to leave. Just then the doctor came into the room, holding a file, and looked at me over his glasses.

"Hello, young lady," he said. "How are you today?"

"Oh, just dandy," I replied. "Actually I think I should go. There's nothing wrong with me. Except maybe you could give me a prescription for birth control. That might be a good idea."

He tilted his head to the side, squinting his eyes and looking puzzled. "OK," he replied, and looked back at my chart. He scribbled something on a prescription pad, ripping it off and holding it out towards me. As I reached out to take it, he pulled back and said, "Are you OK?"

"Of course I'm OK," I replied, defiant and suddenly feeling very angry. "Don't I look OK?"

"Tell me how you've been feeling lately."

"Yeah, you know, I'm fine. I mean, I'm not sick."

"Yes, but how are things? How's work? How's your life? Are you happy?"

"What the hell kind of questions are those? Of course I'm happy," I said, my voice shaking and my heart racing. I could feel the tears well up and I choked back a sob. *"I told you, I'm fine."*

He looked at me as though I was some wounded puppy and put his hand on my knee. I flinched, looking at him suspiciously, angry at him and wanting to just run away. Instead, I sat there and looked away.

"Tell me why you're so sad, Tamara," he asked, his voice filled with concern and care.

I shrugged and said, *"I don't know. I just. I don't feel like me. I mean. I'm a fun person. I like to laugh. And. I'm just not me."*

I could feel myself starting to lose control of my emotions so I took a deep breath and swallowed them completely.

"I just don't know what's wrong with me."

I looked at the doctor and dared him with my eyes to say something. He was an older gentleman, probably a grandfather, balding, with grey hair and kind eyes.

The concern on his face was obvious and he said, *"You, young lady, are depressed."*

No. Fucking. Way. My mother had recently told me that she was diagnosed with depression, and there was no way in HELL that I was going to be depressed, too.

"I am NOT depressed," I declared, shaking and fighting back the

tears. "Depression is for weak people and I am NOT WEAK! You're fucking crazy!" I got up and stormed out of his office, wiping away the tears and determined not to let his flaky diagnosis break through my protective shell.

I was tough. I wouldn't break. I was nothing like my mother and I was determined to get through life without anyone or anything holding me back. No one would ever hurt me again and I refused to accept that someone as badass as me, someone who had survived the childhood that I had survived, could be weak enough to suffer from depression.

Nuh-UH! I thought to myself as I walked down the street, pulling myself together and forcing the tears to fuck off.

"I'm tough!" I repeated to myself, thinking of my favourite character, Dally Winston from The Outsiders. "Me and Dally, man. When you're tough, nothing can touch you!"

Yeah, that doctor was a quack, I told myself. I was OK. Deep breath. I was just going through a crisis of identity. Deep breath. Don't you cry, Tamara. You're tough. Don't you *ever* forget that! You are going to live a great life, I reminded myself. Don't you dare cry!! Because if you could everything you went through at home, you can survive anything!

A few weeks later, after a night out with my girlfriends, I drove to a friend's apartment. It was about 2 a.m. and I buzzed him, asking if I could crash for the night. He let me in and I rode the elevator to the 18th floor thinking of how much life sucked. I couldn't figure out why I still wasn't working for a daily paper, why I didn't have a relationship, why my mother couldn't act like a mom, and why I was so alone.

He opened his door and hugged me, asking if I was OK.

I said I was but that I just didn't want to be alone. He understood and went to the bedroom to get a blanket for me so I could sleep on his couch. I went out to his balcony and looked out across the river at the night skyline of downtown Edmonton, watching the lights twinkle and wondering if I would ever be able to figure it out. Since I was 12, I knew I was going to be a writer and when I started high school I was determined to be a sports writer. There was no other option for me because if I couldn't make my life happen on my terms, I would fail, and failure was not an option.

I was sick of feeling so alone.

I was sick of feeling like I had nothing.

I was sick of fighting to survive.

I was sick of feeling like I had to keep fighting.

I started to cry, leaning on the railing of the balcony and feeling the weight of the world collapse on top of me. I looked down at the ground below me, few cars out at this time of night, and I saw myself giving in and just falling, wondering in those brief moments before I hit the ground if anyone would miss me.

"Your grandfather's heart would break. He would miss you," were the words whispered in my ear.

Holding my head in my hands, I rubbed my temples with my thumbs and closed my eyes, taking deep, slow breaths before looking around to see where the voice had come from.

I was alone on that balcony with only a gentle breeze to keep me company.

My thoughts drifted to my grandfather and I knew he was the only person in the world at that moment who truly loved me, and I clung to those words, knowing I mattered to someone.

With that thought, I went back inside and closed the

door. To this day, I don't know what I would have done if I hadn't heard those words. Was it in my head? Perhaps, but I believe it was one of my guardian angels whispering a message I needed to hear at that exact moment.

The summer after Keon died, I sat at my grandma's grave sobbing, completely breaking down, telling her I couldn't take it anymore, that I didn't want to feel so much pain and stay stuck in the life I was living.

"I'm so tired, Grandma. I'm tired of feeling like such a loser, I'm tired of working at such a shitty job, I'm sick of being alone. I just wish I knew what to do and I wish you were still here," I sobbed. "I don't want to feel like this anymore, Grandma. I can't do this. I'm giving all of this grief and sadness to you to carry because I just can't."

I sat there and just let the tears flow. I couldn't stop them even if I wanted to. My body shook with grief, sadness and so much exhaustion from carrying the heavy burden of the life I had led to that point. I wanted so much more for myself but I had no one to talk to, no one to ask for help, and no one who understood what I was going through. I didn't even understand what I was going through. I was completely lost and felt hopeless. I had no one in my life who could guide me or take away the pain except for my grandma and she wasn't even there to talk to.

I felt so stupid as I sat there but didn't care anymore. I didn't care who saw me talking out loud, sobbing uncontrollably and probably not making any sense. I didn't know why I was so messed up. All I knew was that I was tired, so very tired.

I closed my eyes as the tears subsided and took a deep breath. I wasn't even going to ask "Why me?" anymore. I didn't care. I just wanted someone else to take care of me. I wished I had a mom who was capable of that.

When I was finally able to compose myself, I got in my car and drove home, thinking of ways I could make my life better. I wanted to get out of Edmonton but I was going to stay on my path to be a sports writer so I had to find a job that would align with my dreams.

The next day, I went to the library and casually browsed the aisles, not really knowing what I was looking for or why I was even there.

I wandered upstairs and found myself staring at a section filled with daily newspapers. I looked at them and wondered where I would want to live if I didn't live in Edmonton. One masthead immediately caught my eye, and I picked up an issue of *The Okanagan Sun.*

Hmmm, Okanagan, I thought. Sounds fancy!

I looked inside and wrote down the publishing information with the fax number. I decided then and there that I would be working in the Okanagan because it sounded cool!

I went home and worked on my resumé then sent it off using the fax machine at *Sports Scene.* I had it in my head that my new life would take me to the Okanagan and I was determined to make it happen.

About a week later I got a phone call from the sports editor who said they weren't hiring but that he liked my resumé and would keep me in mind.

About a week after that, he called to tell me a position had just opened up and if I was interested, they would do a phone interview.

Was I interested? Uh, hell yeah I was! I decided that before I could completely move on with my life, I needed closure on one chapter that I had never ended: Keon.

I called his mom and asked if I could come and visit her, telling her I needed to finally meet her.

"Of course!" she responded.

I spent two days with her, listening to stories and looking at pictures. I sat in his room and quietly spoke to him, telling him about the new life I was about to embark upon and thanking him for coming into my life when he did.

I held his pillow to my face to muffle the sound of my whimpers, allowing the tears to flow and wondering why I had to lose one dream in order to make another dream come true.

His mom invited me to join her at church, telling me it would help me say goodbye. I was reluctant because I hadn't been to church since I was an altar girl when I was 13, but she insisted it would heal my heart. I agreed only because I didn't want to be disrespectful, and it turned out to be the best decision I could have made.

The joyous gospel choir touched me in a way no other church experience ever had. The energy in the room was electric and energizing, and I could physically feel the weight of everything I had carried up to that moment, flow out of my body.

While everyone around me was standing up, clapping and singing, I collapsed into my chair, releasing all of the sadness, anger, hatred and darkness I was carrying. His mom put her arm around me, consoling me and telling me to let it all out. I had no control over my emotions; I poured everything out in that moment.

When I got back to Edmonton, there was a voicemail on my machine asking if I was able to fly out to Kelowna for a face-to-face interview for the sports writing job.

Life as I knew it was about to change forever. And finally for the better.

I got the job.

I was about to move away from my mom and distance myself from the demons that had relentlessly followed me. I was given the chance to hit the reset button on my life and launch into the career I had always dreamed of! I couldn't believe my luck.

I thought back to when I first left home and could pack everything I owned into a black garbage bag. By the time I moved to Kelowna, I had to rent a 15-foot moving truck, towing my car behind it. The drive from Edmonton to Kelowna took me through the Rocky Mountains and I don't know if it was naivety of thinking I was invincible or the ignorance of not knowing how treacherous the trip could be, but somehow I made it in one piece.

I had never driven outside of the city limits so taking a trip to another province driving a huge-ass truck filled with all of my worldly possessions and my Chevy Cavalier hitched to the back was a fairly big deal.

Settling into my new life was easier than I thought it would be. I had literally gone from working at a free rag you pick up at a rack as you leave the grocery store to sitting at the sports desk of a daily paper. Take that, I thought, sneering to myself as I remembered my prof's last comment to me.

One day, I wandered down to sit in front of Lake Okanagan with a coffee in hand and looked out towards the mountains. I found it hard to believe I was living the life I had always dreamed of. In fact, part of me was afraid someone would see past the image I was projecting right through to the real me and say, "You're a fraud! You don't belong here!"

As much as I loved the life I was living, I couldn't help but go back to Edmonton to see my friends and visit my mom. I would leave work at 11 p.m. and drive through the mountains until I got back to Edmonton, usually hitting my mom's house around 7 a.m. I never concerned myself with safety during those all-night drives. I was invincible, coffee in one hand, other hand on the wheel and a mix tape of R&B hits to keep me awake.

"Let's go for a drink, my girl," my mom said.

"Where?"

"The Crummydale!" she gleefully declared.

Cringing, I replied, "Ugh, I knew you would say that."

I took her to the Cromdale, the place she spent most of her nights working when I was growing up. The Cromdale was the epicentre of the neighbourhood we had lived in and infamous in Edmonton as being a hub for criminal activity, murders, drug deals, prostitution, gang wars and so much more.

If you wanted to get into that life, the Cromdale was the place to be.

I didn't belong there and neither did my mom, but she felt comfortable there. Maybe it brought back fond memories of her younger days when she worked there or maybe she felt special there. I don't know. I didn't care, either. My only goal was to not get gang raped in a washroom or end up with hepatitis from drinking out of a glass. Seriously, I didn't want to touch anything or anyone. I looked around, disgusted, and thought I would never be like the people in that bar.

And yet there I was, having a drink with my mom.

The Cromdale Hotel was not a nice place. It wasn't a place where dreams were made.

The walls held stories of rage, violence, pain, sadness and even death. The decor was as dark as the souls that lived there.

The carpets were stained with the lives of those who walked upon them.

The tables were unsteady and worn.

The chairs were feeble and weak.

The bar ran the length of the room to where the band played. Saturday afternoon jamborees were a highlight of the week, bringing together people who wanted to have a good time.

Daylight streamed in through the back door, offering

more detail to what the shadows hid so well.

People wandered over to the table to say hi to my mom, curious about who I was because they'd never seen me there before, but I offered nothing more than a fake smile and a dirty look, silently willing them to leave.

No one in that place looked like they knew what a shower was and I couldn't stand to be around them any longer.

"I'm outta here."

"Well, I'm not ready to go," my mom said, clutching her beer and looking away.

"So you want me to leave you here? Seriously?"

"I'll be fine. Go. Have fun. Don't forget condoms!"

Oh my God, she was so annoying! I rolled my eyes and walked out, refusing to make eye contact with anyone and praying to God to let me get to my car in one piece.

My mom and I would repeat this scenario every single time I went back to Edmonton.

It was time to sever the ties with my past.

The Cromdale Hotel was torn down in 2012

Moving to Kelowna, B.C. to work as a sports writer at the *Daily Courier*

Who lets a 22-year-old drive one of these things with her car towed behind it??

THE RED STRING OF FATE

L etting go is easier said than done.

When I was in Kelowna, my only focus was my job. I had no real social life, which was a far cry from my clubbing days in Edmonton. I didn't date and I didn't go anywhere except to and from work. I was fine with my life because I was beginning to feel a sense of security and calm that I had never experienced before. Life was good but I was starting to feel the pressure of my job and second-guessing my ability to be successful in my industry.

One night after work, a group of colleagues went out for beers and invited me to join them. I was the only female in the newsroom, which was perfectly fine with me since I had gotten into sports writing because it was a male-dominated industry and was more than happy to be surrounded by such a cool group of guys. Other people joined the table and were chatting about work when one girl introduced herself as a news writer for a different paper and asked me what I did.

"I'm a sports writer," I replied, sipping my beer and feeling pretty damn good about myself.

She looked at me as if I had said I skinned puppies for a living and replied, "Oh, so you're not a legitimate journalist."

My first instinct was to grab her by the shirt and beat the shit outta her but I knew my colleagues might not find that kind of response endearing, so I glared at her and tried to think of an appropriate response.

"You have no idea, bitch," I replied, getting up and walking over to the bar.

Rage was beginning to be a strong part of my personality and I thought it was simply who I was. I was tough, remember. No one could fuck with me. I wasn't ever going to be someone's punching bag, not physically, verbally or emotionally.

It was no wonder I couldn't make friends in Kelowna. I didn't think I was a bad person but I couldn't seem to connect with anyone. The reality was that I had developed a thick layer of sandpaper to protect myself from the wounds that were starting to fester and seep. I didn't want to think about the abuse but every time I spoke with my mom, memories couldn't help but force their way to my consciousness. I fought hard to bury them again and started taking my aggression out at the gym.

One morning, as I was getting ready to head out for a run, I received an unexpected phone call.

"Tamara, I'm in Kelowna. Come and pick me up at the airport."

What the hell? My grandfather was in Kelowna! I drove to the airport, jumped out of my car and hugged him, refusing to let go. It had been four years since my grandma's funeral and that was the last time I had seen my grandfather.

"I'm so HAPPY TO SEE YOU!" I said, practically screaming at him.

"Calm down already," he said, shaking his head and pushing me away in embarrassment.

"Oh my God, oh my God, OH MY GOD! Why are you here?" I asked.

"I had to come back to Canada for business so I thought I'd pop in and say hi," he replied.

Our reunion was brief but beautiful and I proudly showed off my apartment, my desk in the newsroom and the city I was now calling home. We hadn't spoken about that whole "being kicked out of college" thing, and I was hoping to God that he didn't bring it up. I wanted him to focus on everything I had achieved since then, not dwell on that bump in the road.

"Looks like you've done alright considering you don't have a diploma," he stated, smirking at me across the table as we perused a lunch menu.

I covered my face in complete horror, feeling my stomach drop and glancing up at him over my fingertips.

"I'm so sorry," I said.

He waved his hand, brushing off my reply. "So, what do you plan on doing next?

I had no answer.

"What do you mean, what am I doing next? Jesus Christ, GRANDPA! I think I've done pretty damn well for someone who's

only 23 years old," suddenly forgetting the guilt I had felt minutes before.

"Why do you have to be so God damned defensive, Tamara? You're always on the defence! And so what if you're only 23. You said the same thing when you were 19. "I'm only 19, what do you expect,"" he mocked. "You have to keep trying to do better in order to have a better life. Are you happy living in an apartment or do you want to own something? Happy working as a reporter or do you want to run the show? Quit settling for less than you deserve, damn it."

He knew how to push my buttons, that was certain. The conversation left me questioning myself and my future. I was beginning to wonder if this was it for me. I mean, I had fulfilled every one of my goals so far when it came to my career: wrote for the *Edmonton Journal*, been up in the press box at an Edmonton Oilers game more than once, been in the locker room interviewing NHL hockey players (it was everything I imagined!), and now I was working for a daily paper.

"I don't know what's next for me," I told the news editor one night while we were putting the newspaper together.

"What do you mean?" he asked.

"Well, I've done it all. I've achieved every goal I've ever set for myself and I'm only 23 years old."

"So? Make new goals," he replied, as if it was something I should have already known.

I had no idea what else I could achieve. I thought I had done pretty damn good considering I had been homeless a few years back, but there was no way I was going to tell anyone THAT little tidbit about myself.

I started to envision my career unfolding like this: work at the paper for a couple of years, move onto a major daily paper in Vancouver or Toronto and from there, transition to TV on some sports program. In my mind, it was all mapped out.

Some days, I felt lost and very overwhelmed, tired of feeling torn between my mom and my new life. There were times when she would call me up, telling me about the hardships of not receiving enough money from Welfare. During one of our conversations she told me how she would be getting an additional income from Assured Income for the Severely Handicapped.

"Uh, what?" I asked. "What the hell makes you severely handicapped?"

She began to cry, telling me how she had been diagnosed with depression (duh, no shit, I thought) and that she was emotionally unable to hold a job because of everything that had happened throughout her life.

"Are you fucking kidding me? YOU can't get a job because of all the shit YOU went through?" I screamed at her over the phone. "Unfuckingbelievable! If I can do it, so can you! Stop being such a God damn victim!"

"You're no better than me," she replied. "I don't know why you think you're so high and mighty. Why? Because you're not here? Because you have a job? You don't even have a boyfriend!"

She stopped whining and composed herself. I sat there on the other end of the phone and rolled my eyes, wondering why she was such a pain in the ass.

After a brief period of silence, she said, "Oh, there is someone I want you to meet. He sells bingo cards at the place I play."

Oh my God, she was serious. She wanted me to live her life. I was sure of it.

"Yeah, why don't I do that, mom? Why don't I just move back to the inner city and marry some fucking loser who works in a bingo hall?! Maybe I'll get lucky and he'll beat me, too!"

For fuck's sake, I thought, what the hell was wrong with her? I couldn't even deal with her shit.

A few months later, my mom came to visit me in Kelowna after saving enough money for an airplane ticket. She phoned me from the airport at 8 a.m. on a Saturday morning and asked what I was doing.

"Sleeping, what the hell else would I be doing at 8 a.m.?" I asked, miserable that she had the audacity to call me at such an unacceptable hour.

"Well, get dressed and come and pick me up," she said. I could almost hear her mischievous joy as she said those words, imagining her smile as I replied, "What the fuck? Where are you?" I sat up in bed with my heart pounding, immediately becoming fully alert.

"At the airport," she said. "I was going to take a cab and surprise you but I don't have your address with me," she said, chuckling. "So put some panties on and come get your old mom!"

I sighed deeply, laughing to myself, and hung up the phone after telling her I would be right there. She was full of surprises, I thought to myself. I never in my wildest dreams imagined her coming to visit me in Kelowna but I was excited to have my mom there with me.

She stayed with me for two weeks and it was the best two weeks I've ever spent with her. I would drop her off at bingo and pick her up after my shift at work, and we would sit and talk for hours.

One night, I took her to see *Titanic*.

We got to the theatre and the lights dimmed. My mom started having a panic attack and grabbed my hand.

"I can't be here," she said. "The last time I was in a theatre, some old man groped me! I was just 12 years old." Her voice shook and she was on the verge of tears.

I thought of my own experience in a theatre with my stepdad and how he groped me during a screening of *Mississippi Burning* when I was 14, and became enraged as I shoved that anxiety back down to the deepest, darkest coffin I could bury it in.

I hated him.

I hated her.

"MOM!" I whispered loudly, slapping her hand away. "Smarten up, nothing is going to get you here!" I could feel the embarrassment creep up on my cheeks, flushed with anger and shame. I wished she would just sit down and shut the hell up and forget all of the things that happened to her.

She took her seat and sat quietly next to me. The movie started and the hauntingly beautiful music began to play. I became lost in the characters, and the scars that I thought had healed when Keon died were viciously ripped open. I watched the love story unfold between Jack and Rose and relived the pain of losing him as the movie ended.

I walked out of that theatre a sobbing mess but forced myself to calm down and we drove back to my apartment in silence.

My mom didn't say anything in the theatre or on the ride home but as we sat in the living room, she looked curiously at me and said, "Why did that movie affect you so deeply, my girl?"

Looking up at her, I replied, "Have you ever lost someone you truly loved?"

She shook her head and said no. I smiled softly and said, "I have. And that's why this movie meant so much to me. It was like a message for me to let go."

At the end of my mom's visit, I didn't want her to leave. She had become the mom I always wanted, the mom I remembered when I was little, and all I wanted was for her to stay with me. I wanted her to leave her life behind and start fresh in Kelowna. I wanted to take care of her and she could take care of me and forget all of the bullshit from the past.

But she couldn't.

So she went back to Edmonton, returning to her old habits, and I shifted my focus back to work.

Time passed and the second anniversary of Keon's death was creeping up on me.

Losing Keon became another item piled onto my checklist of things to tell Oprah when I got on her show.

Victim of child abuse. ✔

Alcoholic mother who lived on welfare. ✔

Homeless as a teen. ✔

Death of a boyfriend. ✔ ✔

I made plans to go back to Edmonton for New Year's Eve but this time I was not stupid enough to drive through a snowstorm in the mountains. I booked a flight to leave on December 28 and return January 2. My plan was to hang out with some friends and rock in the new year with a completely new outlook on life.

"You need to meet my boss!" declared my girlfriend.

"Uh, no," I replied, giving her a dirty look. "Doesn't he wear a suit? Isn't he really old?"

"He's 29 and, yes, he wears a suit," she said, laughing at my response.

"Uh, nope. Too old and I don't date let alone date a guy who wears a suit."

I had sworn off commitment of any sort and preferred my mistakes to last for one night. Relationships weren't an option; I had a career to focus on.

That night, I joined my girlfriend and her husband for drinks. The door opened and I glanced up only to see some guy who looked completely out of place in his long, black wool trench coat and fancy shoes. The rest of the guys in the bar were wearing jeans and T-shirts so he definitely stood out.

He nodded to my girlfriend and sat across from me. He wasn't my type at all but I couldn't help but stare at him. He was sexy and there was something about him that I was inexplicably drawn to. I had a feeling that I couldn't let him leave without knowing that I would see him again.

"Hi, I'm Ron," he said, reaching across the table to shake my hand.

My girlfriend was right. Her boss was really hot, even if he was old, I thought to myself. We bantered back and forth all night, and for the next two hours it was as though everyone around us had disappeared and we were the only two people in the world. We talked about everything, sharing secrets and baring our souls in a way that sounds too cheesy to explain.

We were inseparable for the next three days and rang in the new year together. The connection was magical, like we had known each other forever, and I knew I needed him to be more than the casual flings I had preferred. He took me to the airport and I was reluctant to leave.

I knew I had to be at the newsdesk that night but I couldn't stand the thought of not being with him. It was completely baffling and twisted and kind of gross when I analyzed it because the idea of being so connected to someone was *not* in my plans. I was conflicted but decided to trust the universe, this one time.

The idea of not seeing him again scared me and I knew from my experience with Keon that life was too short not to take a chance. As scary as the notion of falling in love was to me, I let myself believe that even I had a shot at a happily-ever-after.

"I met the guy I'm gonna marry," I gushed.

"Uh, you met the flavour of the week," the news editor replied, laughing at me. "I know you, Tamara. You're not the type to settle down."

He wasn't wrong but this was different and I didn't care if it was cheesy and romantic. In the deepest part of my soul, I knew I had met the person I was meant to be with.

The Red String of Fate is an ancient East-Asian belief originating from a legend that two people are connected by an invisible red thread that binds them together, lifetime after lifetime. Your soulmate will come into your life when you need them the most, but it doesn't have to be a romantic relationship; it can be a family member, child, friend or colleague. No matter what happens, the Red String of Fate can never be broken. Western culture has a similar belief called the Twin Flame but I'm drawn to the Red String of Fate because it says you are connected to more than one person and these connections are in the form of love, whether it's romantic or not.

I knew the moment I saw Ron that my soul recognized his and we were meant to be together.

And so we were.

The Monday after we had met, five days later to be precise, we were talking on the phone about everything and nothing.

"I was thinking about you today," he said.
"Oh? What were you thinking?"

"I was in Chapters and saw a card that reminded me of you. It said, 'Absence is to love what wind is to fire.'"

My heart leapt into my throat. "What are you saying?" I whispered.

"That I think I'm in love with you."

All of it was stupid. There was no way we could have fallen in love that quickly and there was no way we would end up married. This didn't happen in real life, right? People don't just meet and know they're meant to be, let alone fall in love and live happily ever after, right?

But we did.

The career I had worked so hard to achieve, bam! Gave it up like that and didn't question myself AT all. I trusted my instincts and decided to start a new life with the man I knew I'd spend the rest of my life with.

"So will you help me look for an apartment when I get back to Edmonton?" I asked.

"Why don't you move in with me?" he replied.

"Uh, what? I ... uh... well, OK!" I said, stumbling over my words and excited about the new direction my life was headed. "Do you have a coffee maker? That's really important to me because if you don't, I'm bringing mine!"

He laughed at my enthusiasm and said that he would make sure we had a coffee pot.

"What about a dishwasher? Do you have one of those?" I was mentally checking off a list of things I needed to have in my apartment.

"I do now," he replied.

I sat there, looking into the receiver and wondering what the hell I heard. Because he did NOT just say that!

"Oh hell no, you did NOT just say that!" I replied. I wasn't sure whether to laugh or reach through the phone and punch him.

He laughed at his joke and my response. Once I realized what a twisted sense of humour he had, I laughed too.

His sanity came into question from his family, friends and co-workers, but we both knew we wanted to be together. It wasn't easy and there were times when we started to question our relationship, not because other people doubted our relationship but because we realized we were such different people.

"I want the red toilet seat cover," I demanded, standing in the middle of a department store and glaring at him.

"Well, I don't. I want the blue one. And why do we even need this stuff?"

"BECAUSE PEOPLE HAVE THEM!" I yelled. "NORMAL PEOPLE HAVE SHIT LIKE THIS!!"

I wanted to cry. We were both freaking out at the magnitude of this life-changing decision to live together and buy pots and pans and other household items only a month after we had met.

He pulled me into his arms as I cried, both of us realizing that arguing about the colour of a toilet seat cover was the stupidest thing ever.

In that first year of our relationship, I went through periods of complete fear of losing him, whether it was from him dying or deciding he couldn't put up with me.

I held onto my belief that I no matter how much I loved someone, they were going to leave. They always did.

"Did you have a bad dream last night?" Ron asked.

"I don't think so," I said, trying to recall if I did.

"You were crying in your sleep, mumbling things," he said, looking at me with concern.

I shrugged. "Don't know. Let's have coffee."

The dreams about the abuse and the violence became worse and worse, and every morning I had to fight to forget. I tried to bury the memories but they resurfaced every night, forcing me to relive the anxiety and fear I felt when I lived at home.

We got married on January 13, 2000, after winning a contest on a local television station. It wasn't how we had envisioned our wedding but I looked at it as a gift from the universe, even though I wasn't entirely sure what that meant. I simply knew that it was another sign that we were meant to spend the rest of our lives together.

"Merry Christmas, Grandpa," I said, calling him up and not caring that it was 4 a.m. in Kuwait. "Remember how you said you'd walk me down the aisle if I ever got married?"

"Jesus, Tamara, what time is it?" he replied.

"Uh, not sure. Anyway, remember how you said that?"

"Yeah yeah," he mumbled. "Merry Christmas, Stinker."

"WE'RE GETTING MARRIED IN A COUPLE OF WEEKS!" I yelled, unable to contain my excitement any longer. "YOU HAVE TO COME HOME!"

He was as shocked as everyone else but happy for us and made arrangements to be there to walk me down the aisle.

The other person I had to tell was my mom. I was truly conflicted because my relationship with her continued to deteriorate. There were times when I would visit her only to return home in tears, frustrated with her spiralling victim mentality. But she was my mom and I reminded myself that she could have given me up for adoption but she didn't. She sacrificed some things to keep me and the least I could do was invite her to my wedding.

"I have nothing to wear," she said, looking at me.

"Well, I don't have any money," I replied, angry with her. "It's always something with you. You need money for food, you want me to buy you cigarettes, you 'borrow' money for bingo. Fuck, mom! Can't you fucking support yourself?"

She looked down and mumbled, "Never mind. I don't need to come to your wedding."

"FUCK! FINE! I will take you shopping but I can't really afford much. GOD!"

"It's OK, my girl. There's a second-hand shop I like."

Did I feel bad that I had to take my mom to a second-hand shop to buy an outfit for my wedding? Yes. And no.

Second-hand shopping wasn't a new concept for either of us although I had phased it out of my life when I became a hot shot sports reporter. You know, because clearly I was too good for that kind of lifestyle anymore. My mom, however, was not and gladly went into her favourite little second-hand shop to find an outfit for the wedding. Twenty dollars and an hour later, my mom walked out with a huge smile on her face and a new outfit to wear at the wedding.

I always said it would be a cold day in hell if I ever got married and it was. No, seriously, it was -26 C and blowing snow in Edmonton. It wasn't a typical wedding because the whole thing took place on TV so I had to be at the station at 5:30 a.m. to get ready. The actual wedding was at 8 a.m., in between newscasts, but I didn't care. I was marrying the man I was meant to be with, and life was nothing like I had imagined it would be.

For once, that was a good thing.

Me, my grandpa and my mom at my wedding

"I think we need to have a baby," I told Ron as we drove home from his parents' 40th anniversary party.

He glanced at me and said, "Um, can you wait until we get home?"

I laughed and said, "Nope."

I went from never wanting to get married or having kids to being blissfully married and ready to have a kid. For reasons I couldn't explain at the time, I felt like this little soul needed to be born.

A few weeks back, Ron and I were talking about the idea of having a kid.

"If we have a boy, we should name him Oscar," he said.
I looked at him in horror and replied, "What the hell kind of a stupid name is Oscar?! Yuck! Oscar the Grouch. Oscar Mayer weiner ..." I started to laugh but saw that Ron was not amused.

"It was my grandfather's name."

I cringed, wondering how much more of an asshole I was than usual.

"Fine, whatever," I said, apologizing. "We're not having kids right now so let's talk about it later."

That night I had a dream about the most adorable little boy with a bowl haircut who was about four-years-old. He looked up at me and said, "Mommy, you're so funny!"

And just like that, I was pregnant.

Oscar was born March 13, 2002, and it was as though my heart exploded with a billion fireworks. I had never been so in love with anyone in my entire life.

"The world is a better place because you're in it," I whispered to him. "It's better because there will be another man just like your dad. You are going to change the world, my boy."

He had already changed mine and I didn't think it could get any better. People would ask when we were going to have another one but I wasn't interested in having more kids.

"I got it right the first time," I quipped. "I don't need to keep trying to have the perfect kid. He IS perfect."

As in love with life as I had become, darkness began once again to creep its way to the surface. I was angry all the time and couldn't find any joy in anything I was doing. My only happiness came from being with Oz. Other than that, I started to become volatile and abrasive for no reason apparent reason.

"You have what's called a chemical imbalance, Tamara," my doctor said. "You've been suffering with post-partum depression, so it's no wonder you've been so angry."

"What the hell?" I replied, in shock. I sat there, flashing back to when I was 21 and the other doctor diagnosed me with depression. It was as though a light bulb popped on over my head and I began to see exactly who I was. "No, you must be wrong I don't want to hurt my kid. I don't have post-partum. I'm just … I'm mad all the time. I hate everyone for no reason. Except Oscar. He is the only person who makes me smile."

My doctor explained that PPD was more complex than what I had thought it was. She told me there are varying degrees of PPD and that my anger was a direct result of the hormones that were raging out since giving birth.

"You're not alone," she told me. "So many women experience this and it doesn't make you weak."

I was just like my mother. I couldn't escape biology no matter how much I wanted to but I didn't have to be like her. My life was mine, not hers, I reminded myself, and I had already broken the cycle of violence by not repeating her patterns.

Time passed and I was determined to prove to myself that I was nothing like my mom. I decided to share my story of growing up in a home filled with domestic violence and abuse after seeing a promotion on a local news show asking for submissions on behalf of the Alberta Council of Women's Shelters. The ACWS was collecting stories about overcoming adversity for a book they were launching called *Standing Together*.

Vivid recollections of the abuse played over and over as I uncovered memories I had locked away and forced myself to forget. It was an exercise that stripped away every layer of protection that I had built for myself and unleashed the demons that I had ignored for so long. As devastating as it was to recall these memories, I was compelled to reveal the truth of my past and hoped that by sharing my experience, it would help someone else heal their own pain.

I was not following in my mom's footsteps or making the mistakes she made; she would always be the victim and I was never going to be a victim again. I also thanked my lucky stars that I had a son and not a daughter. I couldn't imagine having a mother-daughter relationship because, duh, I had such a shitty relationship with my own mom.

That was another reason I didn't want another kid; I couldn't handle the thought of repeating my relationship with my mom. There was simply no way in hell I wanted to be cursed with a girl but, I told Ron, if I had to be stuck with one, she had to have green eyes and black hair like him and she had to be born in November and be a Scorpio.

At least if she was a Scorpio, I'd know how to deal with her simply because I was one too.

My story was accepted and published in *Standing Together,* and six days before the launch party, Lauryn was born. When I found out I was pregnant, I was mentally unprepared and in denial about the situation. I took three pregnancy tests and swore up and down that they all had to be wrong but I knew right from the minute I was pregnant that she had to be a girl.

If you ever want proof that the universe hears you, this is it: Lauryn was born on November 1, 2005, with a head full of black hair and big, beautiful green eyes.

"You're my littlest soulmate," I told her. "I never knew I needed you but you must have known. Thank you for choosing me to be your mom, Lauryn. I swear to God I will never, ever let you be afraid to sleep in your own bed or be scared of me."

This kid melted what was left of the ice around my heart. I told her a story about how she was a star in the sky and she was looking for a mommy. She looked all over, looking for the mommy who needed her the most. One day, she saw me and she knew I was happy but that I needed to heal the pain I had in my soul. She chose me to be her mom and so it was. She became my littlest soulmate.

I named her after my grandma. Well, I gave her a version of my grandma's name to honour her.

And just like that, life changed all over again.

New Year's Eve 2005 with Oscar and Lauryn

ASHES

Happiness is supposed to bring inner peace and gratitude. Instead of seeing the blessings in my life, I began to pick at the scabs.

Nothing felt right. I didn't feel like myself. Outwardly, I was desperate to carve out something apart from who I had become: a wife, mother, friend. I needed to reclaim my identity as an individual. I had allowed myself to go from one extreme to the other: fiercely independent and unwilling to let anyone into my life to opening my heart completely and leaning further and further onto my husband until I was unable to stand on my own.

Writing about the abuse opened the floodgates, and everything I had so carefully buried washed over me like a tidal wave. I couldn't help but remember everything that had happened and I started to drown in the memories. My past blackened out everything that was beautiful in my life and I didn't do anything to stop it.

I despised who I had become and it was no one's fault but my own. It was around this time in my life that I was beginning to examine the details of my childhood and to understand why I had taken the path that I had chosen.

Poor me, right? Amazing husband, beautiful kids, badass memories of a fantasy career ... yeah, life sucked. The problem is, I couldn't see what I had; the darkness consumed me.

My grandfather had finally retired and moved back home, not far away from where we lived. We spent hours together, reminiscing about my grandma and talking about how much she would have loved my kids. We argued about hockey; his unwavering loyalty for the Calgary Flames was impressive, and while I couldn't care less about any team in particular, it was fun to laugh at his passion and intensity as he cheered on his team.

It was nice to finally have someone around who had known me my entire life, and whom I could share stories about my grandma with.

"You're the only thing I have left of her," he said.

"It's weird. I guess you're the only thing I have left to connect me to her, too."

He poured himself a healthy glass of whiskey and looked at me. "Guess we've got each other."

Professionally, I was going stir-crazy. I knew I needed something in my life other than the few consulting gigs I had taken on, so one day I decided to launch a magazine. I developed the concept in April of 2007 and launched the first issue four months later. It was kind of nuts but I felt inspired and everything seemed to fall into place once I made the decision to publish the magazine.

I spent hours at my computer, and some nights Lauryn would climb onto my lap at 2 a.m. while I worked, falling asleep as I tapped away at the keyboard and put the magazine together.

I finally felt like I was doing something with my life that

mattered, you know, other than being a mom.

I craved professional respect and knew that I couldn't be a Betty Crocker housewife so I took all of my experience, injected a healthy dose of my personality into it and published 10,000 copies of the first magazine.

Working took my focus away from thinking about the past, which I was beginning to do far too much of. Sharing my story in *Standing Together* ignited my obsession with analyzing the darkness of my past. I was seeing life differently now that I had a daughter of my own but it was becoming clear that I could no longer hold the coffin shut on those memories.

I felt like I was going to explode but instead I poured all of my energy into that magazine for the next couple of years.

Visits with my mom became less frequent. I didn't want my kids around her; she smoked too much and reminded me of everything I didn't want to be as a mother.

My grandfather had a good relationship with my kids. He teased them, laughed with them, sat and listened to them and brought them sweet treats. When he went outside for a smoke, Oscar would often sit with him and they engaged in strange conversations that made them both laugh.

Some days, I would look around and wonder how I went from being the scared little girl who slept with a blanket over a heater just to stay warm to a woman who was married to the most selfless man in the world and had a fairytale life. I didn't let myself think about it too much because I was sure some devious fairy godmother would appear and take it all away.

So what happens when you put shit like that out into the universe? The universe hears you, and sure enough that asshole of a fairy godmother showed up and zapped my glass slippers into a pair of ugly ass Crocs.

Or something like that.

Actually, what really happened was far worse than I had

anticipated. My grandpa was diagnosed with lung cancer right before Christmas in 2009. Lauryn and I spent every day in the hospital with him, either trying to cheer him up or simply sit there and stare out the window with him.

"Why are you smoking, Great-grandpa?" she questioned. "Smoking is gross and bad for you!"

He laughed and looked at her as he sat in his wheelchair outside of the hospital entrance, puffing away.

"Yes, it is, so you shouldn't do it," he replied.

Lauryn rolled her eyes and I laughed at their exchange. As I wheeled him back to his room, I rambled on about everything and nothing.

"Hey, so this is exciting grandpa," I said, as he lay in his hospital bed. "I was nominated for an award called the Hot Momma's Case Study Project. It's about inspiring other people through your story and resilience. I think I have a good shot."

"So you didn't win," he stated.

"Uh, not yet, but being nominated is still pretty cool," I replied.

"Talk about it when you win."

Taking a deep breath and swallowing my frustration, I tried a different approach to the conversation.

"So I've come up with this concept for an awards program. I want to call it the FIERCE awards. It will be an event where women are recognized for making a difference, whether it's within their own home or on a global scale. I'm really excited about sharing these stories in the magazine! We've already received 25 nominations, Grandpa. The

event will be held in a couple of months, so I've got a lot of work to do."

Instead of replying, he turned on the TV to the World Junior Hockey game. I ignored the fact that he was intentionally tuning me out and continued chattering on about the magazine.

"Ugh, I got some stupid email about how 'offensive' the magazine is, Grandpa. People are so damn sensitive."

I needed to talk about anything other than his condition. I fucking hate cancer. And I refused to give it any power by talking about it, so I continued to rambled on about the magazine.

"People aren't happy unless they're complaining about something." I recognized the irony of my statement the minute it came out of my mouth but kept going.

"You'd think people would have better things to concern themselves with other than my magazine."

He glanced up from the game and looked at me. "You're just like those rap stars, Tamara. You're always offending someone."

I laughed out loud and said, "Aw thanks, Grandpa! I wish I was like those rap stars. I'd be a fucking millionaire!" He shook his head at me, returning to the hockey game.

"You and that mouth of yours," he mumbled. "Offensive!"

He paused for a moment and looked out the window.

"You know, if Canada loses, I'll never get to see them win another gold medal."

I swallowed and took a deep breath, choking back my emotions.

"Yeah, well, they'll win and you'll be fine."

They didn't and he wasn't. He died a few weeks later, holding my hand as he took his last breaths.

His death was my breaking point. Everything I had bottled up – the abuse, losing people I loved, the trauma and the fear – had bubbled dangerously close to the surface up to that point, and when he died, it completely erupted. I almost drowned in my own grief, no longer able to cope. I didn't realize how fragile I was; the whole time I thought I had dealt with my issues, laid them to rest and buried them forever. I thought I was tough, a survivor and a badass. Little did I know that I had simply allowed time to dull the pain and forget the past.

I began blogging about my life, sharing more and more online and offering glimpses into what I had gone through and what I was going through. I didn't share the details of the depression I sank into until after I came out of it because I didn't want anyone to know that it had gotten to the point where I stopped taking Lola to preschool and stayed in bed all day. I had even quit publishing the magazine that I loved so dearly.

Nothing made me happy and everything and everyone made me angry. My responses were harsh, defensive and laced with malice regardless of who was on the other end of the conversation.

"How are you doing these days?"

"Fine. Don't I look fine?"

"It will get easier, Tamara."

"Fuck you. You don't know what the fuck you're talking about."

I became obsessed with trashy reality TV, immersing

myself in the drama and chatting with people online about the scandal of the day. Controversy and turmoil became my drug of choice and I couldn't get enough of it. I looked for it in celebrity gossip sites and engaged in nasty Twitter conversations.

I fed off other negative, self-loathing people and soaked up their energy like a gloriously disgusting sponge.

Negativity filled my entire being and oozed out of my pores, scalding everyone around me. I was blind with rage and drunk on toxic vitriol, spewing venom in almost every interaction I had with people.

Being nasty felt powerful, and I was so damn good at being mean.

Time passed and I completely gave up on myself to the point where one day, I looked in the mirror and didn't recognize the reflection.

I had spent too much time analyzing memories, recalling the most chilling accounts of what I had gone through with my stepdad, forcing myself to confront the memories head-on without digging another hole to bury them in again.

My life had once again taken a sharp left turn and I had no clue how to pull myself up this time.

So I didn't even try.

A few weeks after my grandpa died, I was lying in bed reading, about to fall asleep, when I looked at the doorway and saw my grandfather. I rubbed my eyes, wondering what the hell I was seeing as he walked towards me.

"Tamara, come here. I need to show you something," he said, extending his hand.

"No way, this isn't happening," I said, feeling my heart pound in my chest as my eyes filled with tears. "You're dead, this can't be happening."

"Tamara, get up. Come to the kitchen," he said, grabbing my

hand and pulling me up.

I felt the pressure of his thumb in the palm of my hand as I sat up in bed, crying. I closed my eyes, repeating, "No."

After a few minutes, I opened my eyes and he was gone. I convinced myself it was a dream and quietly cried myself to sleep.

The next morning Lauryn came to the kitchen, looked up at me with her big, green eyes and said, "Great-grandpa was here last night."

I almost choked on my coffee. "What?"

"Great-grandpa was here last night," she repeated. "He woke me up and we went to the kitchen to show me Great-drandma."

I sat there, trying not to cry and wondering how the hell this was happening.

"They said how much I was like you and how much they loved you. They said they were so happy to be together forever."

I couldn't stop the tears. I looked at my beautiful daughter in amazement.

"Look," she said, disappearing into her room and reappearing with a bowl. "They got me some grapes!"

She handed me the bowl with an empty grape stem and all of a sudden I remembered the time my dead aunt visited me in my dreams. Except this time I knew it wasn't a dream.

Talking about the spirits of visiting dead relatives wasn't exactly a conversation I could have with just anyone, but I had one friend who had mentioned spirituality in passing. She believed me and we ended up talking about the concepts of life, death, the universe and discussed what we thought our life purpose was.

She watched me spiral into the depths of my depression and gave me two books for my birthday: *The Seven Spiritual Laws of Success* by Deepak Chopra and *Meditations to Heal Your Life* by Louise Hay.

As much as I loved our conversations, I wondered if she knew me at all. I was no hippy-dippy, yoga-lovin', granola-eatin', meditatin' weirdo. I mean, come on! I was a self-professed pervy girl with a penchant for dirty jokes and a love of wine. That, and I swore a fuck of a lot, so to give me a couple of fluffy books filled with "self-help" crap made me want to smack her with them. I rolled my eyes at the gift and shook my head at her.

"HEY!" she yelled at me. "You will like them, you ungrateful jackass!"

I shrugged, taking the books and throwing them on top of a pile of junk in my basement.

A couple weeks later, I received an email congratulating me on being named the first-ever recipient of the Canadian Hot Momma's Project. The same award I had told my grandpa about being nominated for.

"I told you I had a good shot at winning," I yelled, angry at him for not believing in me.

The rage I felt was out of control. Instead of being grateful for the life I had with my kids and husband, I chose to dwell on the grim past I had left behind.

The utterly dysfunctional relationship I had with my mom had suddenly become important to me again, and I found myself being drawn back to her, asking questions and demanding answers about my past.

"Why did you choose him over me?" "Why didn't you believe me?"

"How could you stay with someone who beat the shit out of you for 20 years?" "What the fuck is wrong with you?!"

I hated my mom. I hated her for so many reasons yet I needed to feel some connection to her, probably to soothe my conscience. It was twisted and insane, but insanity was what I needed to cling to because it made me feel safe. The life I had with my husband was too good to be true, my kids were really good kids and I thought I was a good mom to them; I felt torn between my past and my future.

By this point, I was surprised my husband hadn't given up on me. I was doing everything I could to push him away and believed I didn't deserve anything good in my life. He believed otherwise. He believed in me. And he wasn't ready to give up.

There was never a time when I wanted my kids to have a relationship with my mother. I didn't want to subject them to her mind games or toxic environment and I didn't want them to feel scared, violated or uncomfortable so I didn't bring them with me when I went to see her.

"What's the matter? I'm not good enough to see my grandkids?" *she would ask, rolling her eyes and lighting another cigarette.*

"Yeah, something like that."

We would exchange small talk before I'd hit her with the tough questions.

"Why do you need to bring this up all the time?" she demanded. "It's over. Get over it."

Oh. OK. I'll get over it, I thought.

"Because I need to know the fucking answers," I replied. "Why were you such a shitty mother? You weren't always LIKE that!! If you

had left sooner, MY LIFE WOULD BE DIFFERENT!" I yelled, blaming her for every bad thing that had ever happened to me.

It was easy to blame her. She was a victim with a victim's mentality, and she was weak. She was everything I detested about myself and wouldn't ever allow myself to be, so I hated her. At the same time, I had to remind myself that she wasn't me. She didn't have the strength that I had so I had to forgive her, right? She did the best she could with what she had, but that wasn't good enough for me and forgiveness was not in my nature.

Eventually she would break down and cry, sobbing about how many bad choices she had made and how bad she felt.

Yeah, yeah, I had heard the same shit over and over since I left home. I was done buying it.

I used to feel guilty when she cried but eventually I got to a place where I was bulletproof and her tears didn't faze me, her excuses didn't faze me, and her regret didn't faze me.

I didn't care; I wanted answers.

Our brief conversations always ended the same way, and I would leave, frustrated and vowing to never return. I didn't need this in my life and I sure as shit didn't want it in my life.

Months later, when I was at my lowest point, I literally stumbled onto those hippy-dippy, self-help books, tripping over a pile of crap in my basement. Kicking one of them, I yelped in the pain of stubbing my toe and glared at them, resentful for their mere existence in my house. I let the anger wash over me before collapsing on the floor in despair. I held my head in my hands and started to cry.

"Why has all of this happened?" I sobbed. "There must be a fucking reason!"

I was tired of being so angry.

I was sick of feeling like the universe was constantly flicking me in the forehead.

I was pretty sure I couldn't handle any more emotional trauma in my life.

Wiping my eyes and taking a deep breath, I looked over at the *You Can Heal Your Life* book.

"You really think so, Louise?" I asked out loud, hoping for a response. Instead there was silence so I took a deep breath and opened it up the first page.

Those books became a saving grace in my life. I started to practise the daily affirmations and felt like I was given a magic elixir to bring me back to life. I was thirsty for this hippy-dippy positivity crap, seeking out as much information as I could find and drinking in all of the messages I would stumble across online. The self-help, empowerment, spiritual books that I once scoffed at were quickly becoming my source of power, and I was beginning to see them as healing and comforting.

Eventually, I added meditation to my life. I didn't tell anyone because, duh, I had a rep to protect. I was still hardcore and badass; I mean, I grew up in the inner city and survived a lot of shit, so there was no way I was going to admit that I would sit in silence and search for answers. People who did that would get beat up where I came from and I had to remind myself that I didn't live in the hood anymore. I had the white-picket-fence life with the perfect family not the drug-dealers-hanging-out-on-my-couch life. The struggle was real but I told my brain to shut the fuck up and gave into what my soul needed.

During my meditation, I would see words and phrases like "Inspired" "You are safe" and "Believe" appearing before me in white script as though angels were writing before my closed eyes.

At first I thought I was imagining it and shrugged it off

as impossible, but the more in tune I became with my true self, the more I remembered that I did have guardian angels who had always looked out for me.

I began to open my mind up to the belief that there was more to this world than I could see. In fact, I felt more at peace when I allowed myself to release control to the universe and trust that I would be OK regardless of how I felt or what I was going through at that moment.

The small steps I took by reading those books became the foundation for rebuilding my life and reemerging from the darkness.

"What kind of tattoo do you want?" the artist asked.

"A phoenix," I replied. "And it has to be pretty, not some tribal thing off the Internet." I told him about some of the things I had recently been through and how I envisioned a small phoenix being tied into the Red String of Fate tat I already had on my forearm.

"The entire piece needs to be red. You are not a typical client and this won't be a typical design so I don't want to create it in multiple colours. Is that OK with you?"

"Yaaaaaaaas! Red is my favourite colour! You totally get it!" I gushed, gleefully clapping and excited about the idea of honouring my journey with the phoenix.

The phoenix had always been a symbol I was connected to but I never fully understood the power of the legend. Rebirth and rising from the ashes stronger than before seemed to be a constant theme in my life, especially after what I had overcome.

As I came out of that darkness, the light didn't shine for me right away. It was like waking up from a deep slumber; everything was blurry, and I could barely open my eyes or move my body. When I did, I no longer had any sense of identity and was stumbling around in purgatory, battling to let go of my past and looking for some ray of light for my future.

Even though I had planned to produce the first-ever FIERCE awards before my grandfather's death, I had to postpone it because I couldn't even bring myself to get out of bed and be a parent let alone create the type of event I envisioned. The FIERCE awards became my life preserver as I weathered the emotional storm over the next few months, and the first event was held in October 2010. It wasn't anything fancy but it was quaint and cozy and the women who were recognized seemed to enjoy being acknowledged for their contributions to the world. Reading and sharing their stories of resilience and inspiration made me feel like I was doing something right with my life.

As I fought to figure out who I was, who I had become, and who I wanted to be, I was clinging to the idea that uplifting other women might help me stand up again.

"I'm good," I told myself. "Add it to that checklist and keep going."

Victim of child abuse. ✔
Alcoholic mother who lived on welfare. ✔
Homeless as a teen. ✔
Death of a boyfriend. ✔
Thoughts of suicide. ✔
Depression. ✔
Losing my grandparents. ✔ ✔

I was waiting for the checkmate because I couldn't take much more.

Just like I told myself to, I kept going but I was delusional about being OK.

I wasn't good.

I had definitely come out of my depression by using the affirmations and talking myself off the ledge but I was nowhere near "good."

I had merely done what I had always done. I had survived.

After the first FIERCE awards, I turtled back into my depression and let it consume me. Back to the online drama, back to sleeping all day and back to sabotaging my life. Time ticked by and a few months later, someone asked if I would be producing the FIERCE awards again.

"Uh, sure," I said, not knowing if I could do it.

Two months before the 2nd annual FIERCE awards, I had 55 nominees and no sponsors. I had no idea how the hell I was going to pay for the event but I began to feel like maybe, just maybe, there was something special about what I was doing. As challenging as it was to pull the event together, I somehow managed to secure major sponsors about a month before the FIERCE awards and everything fell into place. It felt like the universe was pushing me to focus on something bigger than myself and ultimately pulling me out of my depression.

The night of the 2011 FIERCE awards was magical and I walked around the event feeling the energy in the room and knowing I had created a special event. Women were united in their power and supporting each other in a way I had never seen before.

There were 150 people in that room and the night brought together people who needed to be connected. For the first time in two years, I felt like my life might just have some meaning.

A couple days later, I looked at the calendar and saw that Lauryn's birthday was creeping up.

"Wow, you're going to be five!" I said, wondering where the time had gone.

She tilted her head in confusion and gazed into my eyes. "I'm gonna be six."

I returned her stare and said, "No, no, silly girl. You're going to be five."

She laughed at me before skipping off to her room and yelling, "Six! I'm gonna be six!"

I looked at the calendar.
It was 2011. Duh.
Which meant she was going to be six.
How the hell could I lose an entire year?

"I don't remember you being five," I mumbled, tears rolling down my face.

In between all of the moments of grief, anger, self-loathing and wrestling with the demons from my past, I had disconnected from reality with only brief moments of focus on the FIERCE awards. In that moment with Lola, I finally understood that I had mentally detached from my family. There were chunks of time that I couldn't recall and things I said that I didn't remember saying.

It took my daughter's birthday to force me to wake up and see that I was missing out on the beautiful life that was right in front me and I knew it was time to honour the phoenix within.

Me and
my grandpa
circa 1975

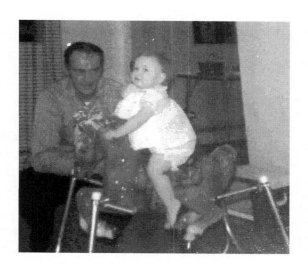

The last picture I have of me and my grandpa. It was taken at my wedding
reception on January 13, 2000

TAMARA PLANT

RISE UP

S o one day, I woke up and everything had magically changed for the better.

Actually, that's bullshit. The truth is, one day I woke up and knew I couldn't go on making the same choices and expecting different results because that would be insane (I saw that on a Facebook post quoting Einstein).

I started to see that I had become a gross caricature of my former self, inside and out, but mostly inside. My soul ached for something more than a Band-Aid fix, and my heart yearned to be free of the armour in which it was encased. All of those spirituality and self-empowerment authors still seemed a little fluffy for my tastes, but I decided to take the messages that mattered most to me and apply them to my life.

Everything from *Notes From the Universe* to quotes posted on Facebook to song lyrics from Eminem, Monica, Christina Perri and Papa Roach became reminders of how strong I could be when I was compelled to close my eyes and give up.

I'd repeat mantras and affirmations, take deep breaths and convince myself that I was on the right path. I wanted to believe that at the core of who I was, there was a happy soul just waiting to be set free, but little things would pop up into my line of sight, clouding my vision and trying to pull me back to the darkness.

Most times, I would respond the only way I knew how: in anger, outrage and by dropping the gloves with anyone at any time.

I started to process the abuse I had gone through as a kid, realizing that it was simply something I had survived and no longer had to be a part of who I was. The abuse didn't define me; I chose what defined me so I decided to focus on living a FIERCE life. The abuse, I decided, was simply a part of my story and a chapter I was going to close.

Forgiveness, however, wasn't about to happen. There was no way in hell I would ever forgive my mom for choosing to be oblivious to what had happened and how she had contributed to my pain let alone let go of the anger I held onto for my stepdad. He sure as shit didn't deserve my forgiveness of his sins, I thought. He could rot in hell before I would ever consider absolution of any kind.

Other than that, I was fine. I missed my grandfather but had finally come to terms with my grief. You live and you die. It's what you do in between that time that matters, and I had decided to focus my energy on creating a community of FIERCE women who uplifted each other and celebrated one another in a no-catty bullshit environment. I didn't want to be a mean girl and I knew that meant surrounding myself with women who wanted the same things so I went about producing the 3rd annual FIERCE awards in 2012, which had an amazing 63 nominees and 275 people in the room.

Around this time, I was asked to speak at a Christmas Bureau fundraiser in Edmonton in front of 650 elite business people and share my story of growing up in the inner city. They had seen a blog I had posted about giving back to charities like Santas Anonymous and the Christmas Bureau because those organizations played a pivotal role in ensuring we had food and presents at Christmas.

Not really understanding what I was getting into, I said sure, and when I stepped up on stage, I saw the mayor of Edmonton and former Edmonton Oiler greats Ryan Smyth and Kevin Lowe. So, like the dork that I am, I started off my speech by telling the crowd that I had to take a picture.

"Say cheese!" I laughed. "I'm pretty sure I'll never get the chance to speak in front of these guys again so I need to make sure I get a souvenir!"

I started speaking more and more after that event, sharing stories of growing up in a home filled with domestic violence and overcoming adversity. I liked the idea that I could inspire others with my story so, as nervous as I was when I was standing in front of the crowd, speaking became another form of therapy for me.

In 2013, I decided to theme the FIERCE awards and call it "Rise Up" after hearing the Beyoncé song of the same name. It seemed fitting, especially where I was at in my life, and that year I opened up the nominations to include both men and women, and was able to celebrate 47 beautiful souls.

The day before the event, I was working on seating charts and organizing awards when I received a phone call.

"Hi, Tamara. Your mom is in the hospital, and I can't get any information because she's in ICU. I don't think it looks good, though. I don't think she's going to make it."

The call was from a friend of my mom's who had known her since I was seven years old and my first thought was, "How the fuck did you get my number?" My relationship with my mom had deteriorated to the point that I couldn't remember the last time I had talked to her.

"Oh," I said, *pausing and unsure of what to say. "So. What do you expect me to do about it?"* I looked around my table at all of the collateral I had for the FIERCE awards and sighed.

"She's your mother," she growled. *"I expect you to go to the hospital to find out if she'll live. They won't give me any information because I'm not related to her."*

She paused before adding, "You know, you owe her. She brought you into this world and the least you can do is take care of her."

"I don't owe her a fucking thing!" I snapped. *"And you don't know what the fuck you're talking about so keep your uninformed opinions to yourself!"*

I hung up, wishing I had a phone that I could slam down onto the receiver. Instead, I slammed my fists onto the table and yelled, "FUCK!"

Knowing that I couldn't live with myself if she died and I did nothing, I jumped in my truck and drove to the hospital, envisioning all types of outcomes.

"You know what, Mom, your timing is really shitty," I said out loud. *"Couldn't pick a different fucking day, could you?"* I swallowed the anger and concern, refusing to feel anything and simply focused on the tasks ahead of me.

"Fuck, Mom, you better not die. I seriously don't have time for this shit."

Under my breath, I whispered, "Please don't go."

I got to the hospital and went up to the ICU unit, sitting outside the locked doors waiting to be let into the ward. The minutes dragged on and I found myself flipping back and forth from things I had to do for the FIERCE awards to wondering if my mom would be OK. Eventually the big, steel doors slowly inched open and I hesitantly walked through, not knowing what to expect. No one acknowledged my presence as I wandered past the main desk, peering into rooms and looking for my mom.

I finally spotted her.

Her hair was a snarled mess and tubes were everywhere, but other than that she looked no different than the last time I'd seen her, which was about six months prior when I had dropped off some of my grandpa's furniture at her apartment.

My kids were with me then and Lauryn had clung to my leg, unsure of what to say or do while Oscar had tried to make the most of it, engaging her in polite conversation. Neither of them wanted to be there and it was the first time that my mom had seen Lauryn since she was born.

"Ah c'mere and give your old grandma a hug!" she told Lauryn, who looked at me with her big, innocent eyes, unwilling to move.

"It's OK, Lauryn, you can sit with me," I said, stroking her hair.

My mom shrugged, lighting a cigarette as I glared at her.

"Really? My kids don't like cigarette smoke. Can you at least wait until we leave?"

She rolled her eyes and stubbed it out in the ashtray. "Oh, I'm so sorry!" she replied sarcastically.

The memory flashed as I stared at her through the glass of the hospital room before a nurse asked if she could help me.

I smiled grimly and said, "No, but I'm hoping you'll help my mom."

She looked at me and referred to her chart, asking if I was her daughter.

"Yep, that's me," I said.

She explained that my mom had kidney failure and that they weren't sure if she would make it but they were optimistic. It was touch and go, she was extremely unhealthy, the nurse said, and I needed to answer a few questions.

Fuck, I thought. I don't have time for this. I closed my eyes, took a deep breath and wondered why the universe decided to fuck with me every year before the FIERCE awards.

"Fine. Let's get this over with," I replied. I was led to a room with a social worker who looked worn, tired and older than my mom. She reached out and lifted my forearm for a closer look, asking about my tattoo.

"Uh, it's a phoenix," I replied awkwardly, hating it when anyone felt the need to touch my tattoo. She remarked how unique it was and how she'd never seen anything like it before.

"Yeah, right, so about my mom," I nudged her, shifting the conversation. "What do you need to know?"

"Well, in circumstances like these, we need to know the medical history but more importantly the family history."

Ah fuck, you're kidding me right?? I do NOT have time for this shit.

"What do you need to know?" I replied, taking a deep breath. "I have a pretty fuc ... uh ... dysfunctional family."

She tilted her head slightly, taking pen to paper and smiling sweetly at me. "Go on," she encouraged.

"Well, look, it's like this. My mom's made some really poor choices in her life and, as a result, treated herself like she doesn't deserve anything better than the way she has been treated.

"She was in an abusive relationship for, like, 20 years. She drinks, she smokes, she has asthma, I swear to God she's bipolar and I'm sure she's got a fucktonne of other health issues.

"My grandma died of lung cancer when she was 57 – oh, and my mom is 56 – so ... there's that. Her real father died of stomach cancer like a billion years ago or, at least 25 years ago. And her stepdad, my grandpa, died a couple of years ago from lung cancer.

"I don't have a real relationship with her, and the only reason I'm here right now is that I got a phone call from a friend of hers to tell me she was here. I have a major event coming up tomorrow that I produce and I don't have time for this!"

I took a breath and looked at her, then looked away when I saw the sympathetic gaze. I didn't want her sympathy. I didn't want anything but to get the hell out of there.

"Well," she said, shuffling her papers, "That certainly gives me a lot to work with. So who would we rely on to discuss your mother's health with if we needed to?"

"Uh, me," I replied. "I'm the only one in her life who has their shit together and can answer any of these questions properly, but here's the thing. After my event tomorrow, I'm leaving for Toronto for four days so unless she dies within that timeframe, I don't want to hear from you."

She looked at me with so much pity that I wanted to walk out. Instead, I said, "Look, I know how this is coming across but I've been in situations like this before with my mother where I've dropped her off at rehab, picked her up from rehab, taken her to the hospital, tried to help her, cried because of her and now ... "I shrugged helplessly, "Now I finally have something good in my life to focus on, and the day before the FIERCE awards SHE GOES AND DOES THIS!" I yelled angrily, holding my head in my hands, trying not to lose control.

I felt her warm hands rub my shoulder, which only made me want to sob uncontrollably, but I took a deep breath and regained control of my emotions.

"I'm fine," I said. "I have to go. If anything comes up, please call me. If not, I will check on her next week."

With that, I walked out of the room and took the elevator to the main floor, purposely taking deep breaths and biting my tongue in hopes of not letting that dam break.

I got to my truck and sat there, finally letting go of the anger, fear and frustration I had felt in the span of three hours.

"Pull it together for fuck's sakes," I told myself. "You have an event to focus on."

The FIERCE awards went off with only one glaring mistake: I had waaaaaaaay too many martinis and made a complete ass out of myself at the end of the event. Unfortunately, my dumb choice took some of the shine off what should have been the best event yet, and all of my hard work into the FIERCE awards became shadowed by my drunken speech.

Sigh. As hard as I was trying, I couldn't seem to get my shit together and no amount of positive affirmations could erase my guilty conscience. Between the guilt of not wanting to take care of my mom and how bad I felt for making such a complete ass of myself at the FIERCE awards, I just wanted to crawl under a rock and disappear. Instead, I left for the conference and tried to forget my stupid mistakes.

I checked in with the hospital every day for a week and each time it was the same: no change. A couple of days passed and I called again.

"She's been released," the nurse said.

"Uh, what?"

"She was released a few days ago. If you need to get in touch with her, I suggest you phone her at home."

I was happy to hear that my mom had recovered enough to go home but surprised that she didn't call me to give her a ride from the hospital.

In the car, nn the way to take Oscar trick or treating, I decided to give my mom a shout.

"Hey, Mom, glad you're out of the hospital."

"Yeah?"

"Uh, yeah. How are you feeling?"

"Fine. Why do you care?"

"Uh, because I'm your daughter and don't want you to die. What the fuck kind of question is that?"

"Whatever. I know you were mad at me for getting sick. You think I wanted to end up in the hospital? You think I did that on purpose?"

"No. I went there when I found out you were sick, you know. I could have given you a ride home, Mom. I didn't expect you to take a cab from the hospital."

"Look, I don't need anything from you. Stay out of my life and I'll stay out of yours. And when I die, I don't want you at my funeral."

"Oh yeah? Well guess what, Mom. I'm glad you didn't fucking die! Now I'm going to take my kid out for Halloween because that is what a good mom DOES!"

I hung up the phone and looked in the rearview mirror at Oz. His eyes were wide and he simply returned my gaze.

"Sorry, kid. Bad timing, huh?"

"It's OK, Mom. I love you."

Time marched forward and I continued to work on transforming myself, often posting reminders on Twitter to stay positive and ignore the bullshit around me. Right before my 39th birthday, I decided to start writing a book about my life and transformation, thinking that maybe, in some small way, someone would find inspiration from what I had gone through.

People on Twitter seemed to think my musings had some depth to them and I had built a small online following that encouraged me to get my story out.

Opening up Google Docs, I started a new file and began pouring out memories, ideas and my perceptions of empowerment, resilience and spirituality. Most of it was a jumble of tweets and ramblings, but sometimes I would sit in silence and let the messages flow through me.

After ripping open every scar, scraping away the thick coats of anger, pain and sorrow, and washing off the remnants of who I had become, I was ready to be the person I was meant to be. No more drama, no more lurking in the shadows and no more holding onto my past. It was time to let the light renew my spirit and heal my heart.

Writing became the real therapy and every time I focused on the book, I understood why my life unfolded the way it did and why I had gone through all of that shit. I was also beginning to see my mom in a completely different light, and although I didn't want to reconnect with her, I understood that her path was connected to mine. I started to wonder about the Red String of Fate and pondered whether our soulmates could be people who came into our life to teach us something specific, good or bad.

Maybe, I thought, my mom was one of my soulmates and that we were in each other's lives for a reason. What if I was supposed to teach her how to be strong and she was supposed to teach me how to forgive?

Well.

Forgiveness was a stretch but maybe she was supposed to teach me how to let go? Or detach? What the fuck was she supposed to teach me? She sure as shit taught me how not to be a mom, I thought. Ugh, nevermind. Maybe I was getting sentimental in my old age, I reflected with a shudder.

Life and work would get in the way of writing, and I eventually lost interest in the book. I had decided that the 2014 FIERCE awards would be my final event, so after Christmas I began taking steps to wrap up that chapter in my life. After the success of the Rise Up theme, I thought, "Hmm ... what do people do after they rise up? Aha! They soar!"

I was about to soar, too! I could feel it in every fibre of my being. I had finally shed layer upon layer of the old me, leaving behind the pain and anger as I shifted my mindset towards love, light and happiness. When I told myself I was good, I actually believed it. Sure, you know, I would have the odd moment of anger or annoyance but, what the hell, I'm human so I didn't beat myself up over it.

My kids were amazing and loved me in a way I had never imagined anyone would love me.

Glancing at the calendar, I realized it was my mom's 57th birthday and had a fleeting thought that maybe I should call her. You know, to make amends or something. She was my mom, after all.

Nah, I'm good, I mumbled and carried on with my day. The next morning, I woke up to this text message:

"Tamara, call me. It's about your mom."

I looked at my phone and my heart sank as I realized what the message meant. I waited for a few minutes before replying.

"Why?" I replied.

"She died yesterday. Just thought you should know."

I sat there looking at my phone, enveloped by the silence, and sighed.

"Of course she did," I muttered.

I wasn't shocked or caught off guard but I felt a sense of loss that I couldn't explain. I knew that phone call wour be our last conversation but I never expected her to die so soon after it. It's wasn't like our relationship was ideal or that we were close or even that I would miss her because I wouldn't. I had already mourned her death from my life years before but I felt such a heavy burden of grief and wasn't sure how to deal with it so I opened up that Google Doc and started typing.

It's easy to be on the outside looking in on someone else's despair and offer advice or to be on the other side of your own tragedy and know how you would handle things differently should the situation arise again but it's when you're in the midst of adversity that it's the toughest to remember everything you know.

I know the things I should do, the way I should handle my emotions and I have the tools I need to deal with grief and with being at the lowest point I've been in a long time but drawing on that knowledge and putting it into motion is tougher than it sounds.

It sucks being here.

It sucks knowing that I KNOW what to do and yet I feel like crawling under the covers and never coming out.

I fluctuate between wanting to give up and wanting to just get past it already.

I'm scared, sad, frustrated, angry, tired and most of all pissed off.

I don't want to hear words of encouragement or have someone try to make me laugh. I don't want to talk or listen to other people tell me their problems, trying to take my mind off my own.

I want to quit.

I want to run away.

I don't know WHAT I want.

I feel very lost right now so any words of "This too shall pass," or "It won't last forever," or "You'll be OK" do not help me right at this exact moment.

I know it won't last forever.

I know it will pass.

I know I will be OK.

But in THIS moment I am not OK.

If I saw someone in the position I'm in, I would offer words of advice like, "You control your emotions; your emotions do not control you."

Do you know how fucking stupid that sounds to someone who's hurting? Or someone who's depressed?

This is for me. In the midst of everything I'm facing and everything I'm going through, I am writing a guide for me on how to get back to FIERCE because it is so easy to talk about being strong when you're not in the vortex of an emotional tornado wishing you would end up somewhere in Oz.

The official cause of her death was a heart attack, and on the day of her funeral, I sat in my kitchen and said goodbye. Going to her funeral wasn't an option and would only create unnecessary drama for myself. I didn't want to see relatives that I hadn't seen in 20 years and I had no interest in reconnecting with anyone. Instead, I sat alone at the kitchen table and started to cry. My tears were for all of her suffering during her lifetime and all of the bad choices she had made.

"Why weren't you stronger, Mom?" I said to my coffee cup, looking around and wondering if she was there with me. "I'm sorry for blaming you for everything. I know you didn't know any better, and when you did it was too late.

"I miss you, Mom. I miss the mom who used to smile and sing along with Meatloaf and Trooper. I miss the mom who loved me when I was little and I looked up to because you didn't care what anyone thought of you. I miss that mom. I miss you."

Taking a deep breath, I realized that my mom died almost two years to the day that my grandpa had passed away and I slumped over, sobbing.

All I wanted to do was to forgive her but I had no idea how to do it, so I simply wiped my eyes and whispered, "Rest in peace, Mom. You've earned it."

"My girl."

I sat up and looked around. No one was in the house, but I looked over to the hallway and felt someone watching me. Chills surged throughout my body and I stared at the door frame.

"Mom?"

Silence.

I closed my eyes as my heart pounded in my chest and tears streamed down my face. "Mom?"

More silence.

I knew she was with me and, although I couldn't see her, I felt her presence and she was as real to me as if she were physically standing there. At the core of my soul, I instinctively knew that she needed me to forgive her as much as I needed to forgive myself. A weight was lifted off my heart as I sat there, feeling like some cosmic light switch had been flipped to "On" and everything became crystal clear. Before she could move on, she needed to make amends with me and, in turn, heal the wounds of both of our lives.

"I'm so sorry, Mom," I said, the sorrow draining from my body. "I love you and know that your life wasn't easy and the choices you made were not always the best but they were yours to make."

I looked over to the doorframe wishing I could see her just one last time but no amount of wishing or being in touch with her spirit would make it so. Instead, I continued talking.

"I get it. I know that I fucked up in our relationship and that I held onto anger for things that you did. You made mistakes and I learned from them. I learned a lot from you, Mom, and I am glad you were my mom.

"I feel like I must have chosen you before I was born, maybe to come into your life to help you in some way and to learn from you in so many other ways. And maybe this is the greatest lesson I'll ever learn from you, Mom, and you're not even here to teach it. I forgive you."

I sat there no longer able to speak as the tears took over.

"I'm sorry," a voice whispered. "I need you to forgive me. And I need you to forgive yourself."

Deep, heavy sobs racked my body as I heard those words.

"I don't know how." I broke down, allowing every emotion to flood my entire being and no longer wanting to hold onto any of the anger or pain I had carried with me for all those years.

I could feel my mom there, smiling at me with her beautiful smile, both of us knowing I would be OK. I may not have had the tools to forgive myself but at least I knew it was what I had to do to finally rise up and soar.

Me and former Oilers' superstars Kevin Lowe (l) and Ryan Smyth (r) at the Christmas Bureau Face Off Against Hunger Luncheon, December 2012

THE ART OF KINTSUGI:
REPAIRING A BROKEN SPIRIT

Turning points can be serious game-changers, and if you're smart enough to learn the lesson the first time you're smacked with one, you can change your life for the better. I, however, am not so smart. It took all of the trauma, twists and turns cumulating with the death of my mom to start to make a difference in my life. It was time to learn the art of forgiveness.

Forgiveness became my second favourite F word. The word no longer meant an absolution of sins; instead it took on a healing power I never imagined. Don't get me wrong, I didn't run around yelling, "I forgive you!" to everyone who had come into my life and left a scar. Also, I wasn't oblivious to my faults and knew that I had to make peace with a lot of mistakes I had made and people I had hurt along the way.

It's not easy to admit that you have caused others pain or let go of the guilt you feel but it is instrumental in freeing yourself from the past and walking the rest of your journey on a lighter path. Forgiving yourself is the single, most freeing gift you can give yourself.

Since my mom wasn't physically here, I had to have many quiet conversations with her when I was alone and felt her presence. I cried a lot during those talks, releasing the anger and resentment with each tear. Let me tell you, there were more than a handful of those sessions, and each time I had one, the lighter I began to feel. It might sound weird, you know, talking to a dead parent and walking yourself through some kind of therapy session but it was the most liberating experience I've ever had.

So how did I get there? It's the million-dollar question with no straight answer. Let me tell you this: there is no right or wrong way, no single perfect solution and no step-by-step guide to forgiveness. The key to forgiveness is your willingness to heal yourself and understand that you are not saying, "It's OK that you were a dick to me" or something like that. Forgiveness is a process and it sure as hell doesn't happen overnight. You won't say, "I forgive you!" and expect your heart to heal like it had been touched by a sorcerer's magic wand. You will say, "I forgive you" and experience a range of emotions as you release the pain you held onto.

The moment I told my mom that I forgave her and meant it, a weight lifted from my life and light entered through every scar I carried with me.

"I don't understand how you can forgive her after everything that happened," a friend texted me after I shared a blog that I had written about my mom after she died.

"Well, what was I supposed to do?" I replied. "Carry all of that anger around with me for the rest of my life and suffer or realize that she did the best with what she knew at the time? I chose to make peace with her and myself."

The word forgiveness is thrown around loosely and has a million different uses in life:

Your kid breaks your favourite vase. No problem, I forgive you.

Best friend spills wine all over your new white skirt. Screw the skirt; let's discuss this wine you just spilled! But, no problem, I forgive you.

Idiot in the parking lot backs into your car and doesn't leave a note. Grrrrumble, call your friend and bitch about the idiot who dinged your car. One week later, you forget about it. Does it need forgiveness? Sure does! Otherwise you are hanging onto that anger and the nameless idiot who didn't have the common courtesy to take responsibility.

Go deeper and maybe forgiveness applies to someone who has truly wronged you and negatively affected your life in a way you simply can't imagine forgiving. After healing my relationship with my mom, I told myself a hundred times over that I could forgive my stepdad for what he did too. I mean, I had compartmentalized the abuse and rationalized that it was a part of my journey, something I had to go through to get to where I was.

It was over, I lived and was absolutely fine. Just like everything else I had gone through, it all had a reason, a greater plan than I couldn't see right now. All of it was a part of my journey and I learned to accept that although my path was not an easy one, everything I went through was part of a greater plan.

That's what the spiritual masters teach; we choose our life path before we enter this realm, and whatever struggles or encounters we have are predetermined. We choose it because we can handle it so, stupid me, I chose this lifetime and I had to damn well deal with the consequences of that choice.

You know that list I was using to keep track of all the crap in my life? That was a stupid thing to do. By maintaining a checklist of all of the drama, pain, losses and moments that changed my life, I invited so much more of that shit into it.

When you expect bad things to happen, don't be surprised when they *do* happen. Once I got rid of that list I was able to invite what I really deserved into my life: love, happiness, freedom and light.

I began to delve further into the spiritual teachings to explore the angel side of things because I always felt like I had a guardian angel watching over me. I believed in reincarnation and angels and spirits. I mean, come on, I had enough ghost visits from dead relatives to make me a believer.

One afternoon, I was chatting with a casual acquaintance who was also deeply spiritual and was telling her about my experience with my mom and how weird it seemed that I could really forgive my mom.

"Forgiveness is your life purpose," she said.

I stared blankly at her before laughing out loud. "No. You don't understand. I don't forgive and I don't forget. It's kinda been my thing over the past 38 years. I've never forgiven anyone for anything. My mom was the first person I've truly been able to forgive."

She smiled warmly at me and I could feel myself starting to cringe. "You have free will so you can do as you please but have you ever considered that forgiveness could be why you chose this lifetime? Why you went through everything you did and have come out of it stronger than ever? Forgiveness is your life purpose."

I could feel the grimace twisting my face and I shook my head, defiantly refusing to listen to her. "Yeah, no. I think no. Forgiveness is not my thing. I mean … yeah, definitely no."

I could forgive the little things, the things that really didn't matter, but when it came to forgiving my stepdad, I struggled. When I was awake and thinking about it, I could say, "Yeah, sure, I can ***air quotes*** forgive him."

When I slept, my subconscious mind would unlock the demons and I became that same terrified, cowering little girl who hated him. Nightmares were a bitch and I could feel the rage flood my heart and course through my veins whenever I had one. I couldn't hide my true feelings when I was asleep and I would lash out in anger at him, wanting only to see him suffer.

When I woke up, I was so conflicted with how I felt and how I wanted to feel. I didn't want to hate so vehemently but clearly I wasn't ready to let go of my pain so I buried it again and forgot about him until the next time I slept. I only had one F-word for him and it definitely wasn't forgiveness.

Once I embraced the idea of forgiveness, I opened myself up to other things like "letting go" and started peppering my thoughts with words like gratitude, abundance, prosperity and trust. I decided it was time to start living again and the only way to do that would be to shed light on my past so that it no longer held me captive in the darkness.

Being grateful is the easiest thing I've ever done. No matter what you're going through or how much shit piles on top of you, there are a million other reasons to practise gratitude and shift your focus.

Bad day at work and your kid won't shut up? Be grateful you have a job and a healthy kid.

House is a mess and you have to cook dinner AGAIN. You've got a house to live in and food to eat.

Life sucks and nothing goes right? I got nothin'. Except maybe, just maybe, you're attracting some of that into your life, so take some responsibility and make a change.

The biggest mistake I made was dwelling on the "how" of things. How was I going to get to college, how was I going to become a sports writer, how was I going to pay my rent, how I was going to avoid ending up like my mom? I was drowning in the hows. I can look back now and see that the most magical turning points in my life happened when I didn't think about the hows and, instead, simply dared to dream big.

When I listened to divine messages and envisioned my future, doors began to open but when I gave into fear and ego, they slammed shut again.

Doors being slammed in your face are detours to something better. I know this from experience and only found out 38 years into my life that what I had to learn the hard way is something Buddhist teachers have been telling their students for thousands of years. Would have been nice to know this before I went through half the shit that I went through, but I know it now, which makes obstacles and endings a little less painful.

I started tweeting out more and more messages to myself about forgiveness and gratitude and staying positive, a far cry from when I joined Twitter in 2009 and was standing at the precipice of my own great depression. There was understandably some suspicion from fellow Twits who had followed me during that dark time and reluctance to accept that I was emerging from my spiritual coma and becoming who I was always meant to be.

I'm not sure if their refusal to see me for who I was becoming pissed me off more than the fact that I kept having my past anger thrown in my face but I started eliminating people from my life, both online and in the real world. I decided that the only way I could soar would be to get rid of the anchors that kept dragging me down. I stayed as focused as possible and kept talking to myself on Twitter by posting reminders to myself to ignore the drama and focus on all that was good in life.

For some reason, my tweets would resonate with people and I began to get messages of gratitude for what I was sharing. Often people would tell me the messages were exactly what they needed to hear, so I continued to write even though I didn't think I was posting anything overly profound:

> If you're feeling neglected or ignored, maybe the other person is going through something you don't know about #notalwaysaboutyou

> Be forgiving. Not everyone knows your pain. Believe the best in everyone and trust that they WILL find you when you need them.

> You may not be able to save the world but you can start by changing someone's day simply by offering a genuine smile. #beHAPPY

Twitter really captured my evolution from absolutely awful to positively FIERCE and I knew that I couldn't hide from my darkness so I owned it. I know who I was but I also know that I'm not that same person anymore.

Anyone who even hinted at any sort of drama, negativity or tried to hold me to my past mistakes had to go, and it didn't matter if I had known them all of my life or for a few minutes. If you're surrounded by people who want to see you fail, bring out the worst in you or pull you from the path you want to be on, you need to let them go. Severing ties, regardless of their connection to you, is the greatest gift you can give yourself.

But Tamara, you ask, why would you cut people from your life? Why can't you see the best in them, accept them for who they are and see past their drama especially if you expect people to see the best in you?

Well, for me, the answer was simple: cutting people out of my life wasn't difficult. I mean, I was able to keep my own mother out of my life because she wasn't a healthy person to have around, so phasing out anyone else wasn't hard to do.

Also, I didn't want to keep living the way I had been living so that meant some of the people I had allowed into my life had to go. It didn't have to be a dramatic ending or huge blowout, but I examined every single one of my relationships and asked myself, "Who am I when I'm around you?" and "What do we both bring to this relationship?" If I felt any sort of negativity creep into my soul when I thought of the person, they had to go. You know that twitchy feeling you get at the mere mention or thought of someone? Yeah, those people were the first to go. Mostly, though, it was my issues, not theirs, that made me detach from the relationship. I needed to heal and you can't heal yourself with bad medicine. And no, they weren't "bad" people by any means, just not what I needed at that time in my life.

So far, forgiveness, gratitude and letting go had become the greatest themes of 2013, and I was starting to see major shifts in how I was seeing things on a daily basis. The drama and heaviness that had regularly found its way into my life seemed to fade away, replaced with affirmations and a conscious effort to avoid anything and anyone who thrived in negativity.

The more I ignored any controversy or conversation that was filled with negativity, the better I felt. I wasn't oblivious to what was happening in the world or petty drama that people seemed to thrive on; I made a conscious decision to focus my attention elsewhere. For every sad, depressing news story that would find its way into my timeline, I would focus on gratitude. For every mean comment I saw online, I would turn to Doreen Virtue for angel messages.

Angels have always been there, protecting me along my journey whether I knew it or not. My first memory of these divine lightworkers is one in the form of an imaginary friend named Heidi. She was very real to me and I remember her as blonde and fairy-like, surrounded by light and happiness. And no, it wasn't some Tinkerbell delusion because I hadn't even seen *Peter Pan*. Like all imaginary friends, I eventually stopped seeing Heidi and consequently forgot about her, especially when my childhood abruptly ended and my focus became survival.

My first encounter with Doreen was in Canmore, Alberta, the summer of 2010 after my grandpa died. Ron and I took the kids to the mountains for a week and we were wandering down main street, checking things out. I walked into a store called Spirit of the West and felt instantly connected to the energy in the room.

The store was filled with various items ranging from Laughing Buddhas to angels to dreamcatchers and everything in between. I wandered around and was drawn to a table filled with different decks of cards and was compelled to purchase Doreen's deck of "Daily Angel Messages."

I had no idea what the hell angel cards were or how to use them, but they awakened something that I had locked away when I was a kid. Flipping through each card reminded me of the angels I used to talk to when I was little, and I began tapping into the power of receiving messages from the cards.

My soul burst with joy as I reconnected with my angels, and it was another small step on the path of my healing journey. But it was one I kept to myself. I didn't want to anyone to think I was turning into some kind of frou-frou nutcase who talked to the air.

Even though I hid in the spiritual closet, I was beginning to see the beauty in life and the universe was opening the floodgates, illuminating a brand new path for me to walk upon. After dipping into the angel realm, my curiosity got the best of me and I started exploring other mystical authors. I signed up for Mike Dooley's *Notes From the Universe* and eventually opened the Louise Hay and Deepak Chopra books I had received as gifts.

In the summer of 2013, when I thought I was on the other side of my journey, I had the opportunity to actually MEET Mike Dooley in person. Mike was in Edmonton teaching his "Playing the Matrix" course, and although I initially thought the course had something to do with Keanu Reeves, I knew the time had come to figure out my life purpose, so I signed up, giddy with excitement to be in the same room as The Universe guy. I was fairly confident I was meant to do something that inspired other people. I mean, the FIERCE awards seemed to be gaining popularity and it made me feel good to recognize the differences other people were making.

Yup, I thought, I've got my shit together, so it's time to figure out a way to live my own inspired life.

I spent the day with Mike and about 75 other people learning how to live the life we'd always dreamed of. I also paid to go to the private, super exclusive session with him after the conference where I realized just how lousy my confidence was. I had big dreams of writing a book and travelling around the world putting on my own workshops but I didn't really believe I deserved to have them come true. Dammit. I was a fraud. The FIERCE awards were supposed to be about inspiring other people, but here I was, refusing to believe I could do anything to make a damn difference.

I could feel myself shrinking in the midst of all those people who seemed to have it together. BAH! This wasn't the way the universe worked, I thought. I was supposed to quit worrying about the "how" and just envision the outcome but all I could see was me sitting on the sidelines again and twiddling my thumbs. I was hopeless.

I went home that night and looked up at the moon, wondering where all the magic I once believed in had disappeared to.

I've always had a fascination with the moon and used to think that if I looked up and could see the man on the moon, it meant that someone out there loved me. The first time that thought popped into my head was on a bus ride home from visiting my boyfriend, and although that relationship ended when I was 19, my faith in the moon and love never changed.

Over the years my ideas about the moon shifted because I married my soulmate *insert swoon here* and I intuitively understood that the moon has the power to affect energy.

Remember learning in Grade 5 that the energy of the sun and the moon are responsible for the tide? The sun is 27 million times bigger than the moon but it's also 390 times farther away which, according to the National Oceanic and Atmospheric Administration, means that the sun has only 46 per cent of the tide-generating forces that the moon has. The moon is more powerful than the sun in that regard so if it has THAT MUCH POWER, wouldn't it make sense that it can affect your energy when there is a full or new moon? Humans, after all, are made up of between 55 to 75 per cent water.

Knowing this and developing my beliefs in the universe brought me to manifesting with the moon. Like my secret conversations with my angels, I tried to keep my conversations with the moon on the downlow, so one night when my husband asked why I was burning candles outside and talking to myself, I felt like he had caught me having an affair with one of my Hollywood crushes.

"Don't look!" I yelled at him, putting my hand up and turning away in embarrassment. "Get the hell out of here!"

He gave me a confused look and shook his head.

"Whatever, weirdo," he said before going back into the house.

I'm just grateful he didn't lock the door.

Once I started seeing the results of manifesting, I became more and more confident in trusting the universe and planting wishes, not caring if my hubby thought I was kooky. Oscar and Lauryn were intrigued by my moon rituals and started participating.

Finding my way back to spirituality and receiving angel messages was important to me. I also believe the universe listens to you and when you use words like "don't" or "can't," well, guess what's going to happen? You can't and you won't. The universe will make sure of that, not to punish you but because you are asking for it. You must change your words to focus on what you have as if you already have it. "I am" and "I can" are pretty powerful phrases and open doors if you really believe in what you are putting out to the universe.

When I intentionally began using the moon to manifest, I started out small, releasing anger and grief, asking for the strength to forgive myself and to start living my life's purpose. Here's the thing, though. I wouldn't just write down my wishes and burn them on a full moon. Day after day, I would take action steps to change my life for the better, whether that was talking myself off a ledge when I felt like giving up on myself. It is easy to wallow in self-loathing but I chose to open up that Google Doc I had started a couple years before and purge my emotions onto paper.

It's all a process, and change takes time but if you want it – *really* want it – you can change where you are at any given moment. You're not chained to your situation no matter how bad it is. The only shackles that keep you from moving are the ones you place on yourself, but here's the thing: YOU HAVE THE KEY TO UNLOCK IT ALL! No amount of self-help books or inspirational speakers or daily mantras or positive affirmations can change anything unless you get off your ass and do the work. I won't tell you it will be easy but I can tell you it is possible.

I'll also tell you this: there is nothing wrong with you. You may have suffered trauma, experienced a tremendous amount of loss in your life and hit rock bottom more than once but you can take those shattered pieces of your soul and put them back together.

The Japanese art of kintsugi (kin means "gold" and tsugi means "connect") is an ancient form of restoration using gold lacquer to repair broken ceramic pottery. The spiritualism behind this beautiful art is relative to wabi-sabi; finding beauty in that which is broken. How cool is that!?

Although the symbolism of the art celebrates your scars and honours everything you've been through by bringing attention to your past in the most beautiful way, it's also about others seeing the light within you regardless of your past. If someone can see the light that pours through your scars and illuminates the world, they are seeing beyond your mistakes and that in itself is enlightening.

Me and Mike Dooley in Edmonton at the "Playing the Matrix" conference, August 2013

Awakening isn't solely about healing yourself; it's about being able to strip away the need to judge others because you understand that you are not without fault. It's also about releasing the ego which allows you to live your life without chasing accolades or attention or putting your needs above the needs of others. All of this is a process and it needs to begin with repairing your broken spirit.

Kintsugi isn't simply about repairing broken pottery or healing your spirit; it's about taking what's damaged and turning it into a masterpiece.

You have the ability to take everything that has broken your spirit and reclaim your power but it starts with healing each broken part and wearing the gold scars as a badge of honour. You are resilient, you matter and you've got this.

Redemption has always been my favourite theme. Even as a kid I was drawn to movies like *The Outsiders, Rocky* and *The Karate Kid* because I believed in the underdog and thought everyone deserved a second, third and 11th chance. I lost sight of who I was for a really long time, forgetting what I believed in and gave up more times than I care to count. It was only when I stopped fighting and let myself burn to the ground that I was able to renew my spirit and rise up stronger than ever. So what if it took more than once for me to get it right?

Champions don't quit because they're knocked out in the ring; they get up and fight again until they achieve the goal, whatever that may be. For me, inner peace was the goal and living the rest of my life in love and light is the end result. Will there be days when I want to rage out because of a bad day? Yep. But the anger will never be the same as it was and my greatest success in life is knowing my kids will never experience the kind of trauma in their home that I did.

"Lauryn, did you know that you are the first girl in my entire family to start your life with a clean slate, no demons to battle and no trauma to overcome?" I told her one night before bedtime.

"Um. OK," she said, her eight-year-old mind not really comprehending what I was telling her. "Can I get a drink of water?"

"It's a big deal that you'll understand when you're older. It means everything to me that you make good choices and be happy because you have such an amazing opportunity. You, my girl, are born to be fierce and happy and loved and safe."

Call it luck, call it fate, call it good judgment or maybe it was a combination of all three but I was able to break the cycle of domestic violence, and despite the adversity, I was able to make a better life for myself.

My kids have something that I never had: a solid foundation to build their life on. No cracks, no drama, no scarring events, just love.

My mom and my grandma didn't have a painless path either, and I'm sure my great-grandmother, as a proud Cree woman, had her share of challenges, too. It matters to me that my kids grow up knowing they are loved, safe and happy. It's all any parent wants for their kids, right?

I'm fortunate that in my lifetime, I've been graced with earth angels who have come into my life at the right time and taught me the things I needed to learn.

I may not have acknowledged their gifts at the time but I've kept them in my heart and rebuilt my life with each lesson.

Even the people you can't stand or hate are in your life to teach you something and sometimes those are the greatest gifts you will receive. They might seem like your greatest burden but if you look at it as a blessing in disguise, you might learn what you need to know sooner than later.

Life's a journey that you experience more than once, but during this lifetime you have to continually learn and grow and love and lose; it's the only way you'll become stronger and appreciate the good that ebbs and flows from your life.

If you can take one step every day towards understanding that you deserve happiness and that life doesn't have to be filled with pain in order for you to experience joy, you'll be on the right path. Find something to be grateful for every day and release the need to fret about what has no real impact on your life.

I'll always be a work in progress and I'm OK with that. I won't pretend I don't get angry or sad or frustrated because I do. I also have the most twisted sense of humour and love to embarrass my kids. I love to drink wine and watch *Sons of Anarchy* and *Magic Mike* and ogle Hollywood sexpots like Charlie Hunnam and Channing Tatum.

I find great joy in my daily cup of coffee and am constantly awed by the sunrise. I yell at Ron for stupid things that I can't even think of right now because overall he's pretty awesome and I've told him a million times that if he ever leaves me, I'm going with him.

Oscar is currently saving up his money for therapy because I'm the mom who has no problem teasing him about anything and everything, but I'm fairly confident he'll turn out just fine despite my goofy parenting.

Lauryn is rockin' some serious confidence and is happy in her own skin, something that took me 40 years to achieve. I have a family and a happiness I never imagined thanks to Ron and the kids and I know they wish I wouldn't swear nearly as much as I do, but with all my faults they love me still.

I've got a handful of friends who have stuck around during this journey but most of them have left or I've pushed away.

They've all taught me something and I want them to know how grateful I am that they came into my life, regardless of whether they stayed or not.

Since my mom died, I've have the best conversations with her and was told once by a medium that she can do more for me now than she was able to do while she was here on this earth. I believe that, because life has never been better and I know she's watching out for me. And this is how I will always remember her:

As for me, well, I've finally found inner peace and life is beautiful.

One of our many family selfies. This one was taken the summer of 2014 in Canmore, Alberta

EPILOGUE

The universe has a funny way of tying up loose ends even when you think you've turned the page on that chapter of your life and moved on. Right before my 40th birthday in November 2014, I decided to take one last crack at finishing the book I had started way back in 2012. I opened up the Google Doc and wondered how the hell I was going to piece together the 100,000 words I had dumped into the doc when it was a jumbled mess of projectile word vomit. I had collected tweets, written down memories, typed out random thoughts, and compiled one big mess of characters. I had no idea how to turn it all into a book so I closed the doc and, once again, carried on with life.

A month later, after being laid off, I received an email from Hay House about an upcoming conference that was coming to Edmonton featuring Wayne Dyer! I couldn't believe my luck! Maybe it's a sign, I thought! Maybe I'm meant to go to this conference and refocus on what I'm meant to do! Maybe, I thought, just MAYBE this was the universe's way of telling me that I shouldn't give up on my dreams! But what about the loss of income, I thought? Crap.

Maybe I shouldn't spend the money. Maybe I should wait and see if I get a job before I spend a couple hundred bucks on something like this. But I could imagine Doreen Virtue saying, "That's just ego speaking! Ego wants to see you fail so it will give you every reason why things won't work out. You need to trust, Tamara."

So, despite just losing my job right before Christmas and having no opportunities in sight, I spent the $197 on a presale VIP pass for the event, calling it a gift for myself, and tucked it away until May.

One morning in February, almost two years to the day my mom died, I woke up from a dream that had my heart pounding so loudly that I thought I would wake everyone up. I sat at my computer and recalled the vivid imagery of what had unfolded in my subconscious.

Feb. 7, 2015

I have to share something with you. A part of me has been really hesitant to actually go through with publishing this book. If I'm completely honest with myself, I have been a little bit terrified of sharing such a raw look into my journey.

The concept for this book came to me back when I was a kid, going through the things I was going through and thinking that maybe I was meant to live the life I was living because I was meant to share my story. Sounds weird, right? The seed was planted and it wasn't until November 2014 that I actually sat down and started to put the pieces of my life on paper, trying to fit it all together into a book and give it some sort of flow so it all made sense. Over the course of the last year, I forced myself to take another detour, probably one that I needed to take in order to get to the place that I'm in right now, and during that time, I ignored the book even though I kept telling myself that, yeah, I'd publish it then ignore it again.

Once again, the universe decided to gently guide me back to this book. I was given the time to work on it, but my ego kept getting in the way saying, "Who would want to read this?" "Why would your story matter to anyone?" "How can you make a living if you're not working full time but instead you're putting energy into a book that no one will ever care about?"

And my ego won. I kept ignoring the messages I was given by my angels and continued to focus on other things that kept me away from my life purpose. Everyone has a life purpose (not a special purpose like Steve Martin in The Jerk, and if you are too young to get that reference, it's a movie about a very special guy who thinks his special purpose in life is his dick. So, no, not the same type of purpose).

I digress. Fast-forward to this morning. I wake up at 4 a.m. most mornings because I am wired like my mom that way, and read for a while. I scanned the celebrity gossip sites for fun, light news (not the malicious, awful news that hurts people) and eventually fell back asleep. During the hour that I was asleep, I had a dream that I was on a plane going to Las Vegas.

As I looked out the window, I could see the Strip and smiled at the view. I looked at a magazine and saw an ad for the Stratosphere and saw the ride that pushes you outside of the building, suspended hundreds of feet in the air in nothing but a little bucket (or something like that; in my dream, it was a little pod of some sort).

Nevertheless, just the thought of that ride terrified me. I could feel my heart racing and became extremely anxious because I seriously have panic attacks when I'm up high anywhere. Except for planes. I feel quite safe in planes, which is weird. At any rate, the plane became the Strat and I found myself thousands of feet in the air, waiting to get on this ride. When the attendant opened the gate for me to get on the pod, I froze. I couldn't move. I was too afraid to get on because I could see over the edge there were just clouds and miniscule specks below that were cars and people. Even the buildings looked like kids' toys.

I knew I was holding up the line by not moving but I just sat on the step, trying to catch my breath. No one was forcing me to do anything, I simply had to do this on my own.

"You're safe. You're protected. Nothing will happen. You'll be OK."

I kept repeating that to myself until eventually I stepped onto the pod, closed my eyes and trusted that I was OK. My heart was still racing and I could feel the other people getting onto the pod, sitting down and strapping themselves in. I opened my eyes when the pod started to move, feeling the panic set in again and wanting nothing more than to retreat to the safety of a platform that was secure and stable.

Instead, I took a deep breath and called upon my angels to surround me with a white light of protection. I opened my eyes again and began to breathe in the beauty of what I was seeing: the clouds, the buildings, the scenery. I actually smiled as I felt waves of calmness wash over me. I looked to the right and was gifted with the most beautiful rainbow arc that appeared out of nowhere. The ride began its descent and I was in absolute awe of the journey. Everything I was seeing was magical and seemed surreal because I was doing something I never thought I'd ever do.

When the ride reached the ground, I stepped off feeling like there was nothing I couldn't accomplish. I felt confident and strong and courageous but most of all I felt proud of myself for taking the ride.

Obviously I wanted a souvenir of this ride so I wandered over to a gun range (don't ask me why; it was in the middle of the fairgrounds that I had landed in) and asked the attendant if I could have a picture of me on the ride, thinking that there must have been some kind of automated photo at a certain point that would have captured the moment (God, I have weird dreams). She smiled at me and said they didn't have such a thing but if I wanted I could take a picture at the descent point. I shrugged, thinking, "Why the hell not? I need to prove that I actually did this." We walked over to the point where I had exited the ride, and as I looked up, the rainbow I had seen earlier was right in front of me.

"OMG!" I exclaimed. "I need to take a selfie in front of that rainbow!" She smiled at me and offered me her camera. I can still see myself posing in front of the rainbow, happier than I'd ever been and grinning like I'd just won the lottery.

And then.

The rainbow moved across my face and I closed my eyes, soaking up the beautiful energy and basking in the magic of the colours. It was the most amazing experience I've ever had in a dream.

When I woke up, my heart was racing and my hands were shaky. I walked into the kitchen, made myself a coffee and tried to process what I had just experienced.

I took a deep breath and tried to calm my nerves by looking for some kind of meaning to the dream.

I began to realize that I had to face my fear of publishing this book because it DOES matter and it IS needed in the world.

I trust that this dream was a message from my angels because they've tried to give me signs before, especially over the past three months, but I've dismissed them.

I'm not ignoring the message this time. Instead, I'm going to take a complete leap of faith and simply get this done. It's what I'm meant to do.

I used the momentum to plug away again at the book, but it was interrupted by the start of a new job. A few months passed and when the weekend of the Hay House conference came, I booked a room at the Marriott Courtyard in Edmonton, treating myself to a weekend away, and resurrected the dusty Google Doc.

I decided to focus completely on the book. I knew the "I Can Do It" conference would be another turning point for me and I was ready to receive a few gifts from the universe in the form of messages from Wayne and a few other enlightened authors I had never heard of.

Being in the presence of Wayne Dyer was pretty damn awesome. I sat there, in awe, for three hours, soaking up every word and learning as much as I could about how to take everything I had been through and turn it into something positive. He started off his speech talking about sex and I instantly fell in love with him.

"I have sex almost every day," he said. "Almost on Monday. Almost on Tuesday. Almost on Wednesday ..."

It was an endearing way to lighten up the crowd who were mainly there to get in touch with their deeper selves and I loved him more for it.

He told a story about the anger and resentment he had towards his father and it resonated with me because of my relationship with my mom. When Wayne spoke of forgiveness and letting go, I totally got it. I felt like if Wayne and I went for coffee, we could swap war stories of survival and aha moments, talk about how we both believed that we chose this life before we started it, and my mind would explode with admiration and respect for his awesomeness and he would laugh at my inappropriate sense of humour!

What? He had one, too and a girl can dream :D

After his speech was over and the crowd went wild, I ran up to the stage and tried to sneak in a selfie with Wayne. He was handing out books to some of the people in the front row and I had my back turned to the stage trying to get him in the shot. I didn't care if I looked like a total fangirl because I WAS fangirling about being in his presence.

When I couldn't get a decent shot, I turned to face the stage and decided to take a close-up of him. He danced over to me – no, seriously, he grooved to the music and came over to me, so I asked if he would be in my selfie and, sure enough, he indulged me! But I was so nervous and excited that I couldn't steady my phone enough to get a clear shot.

Whatevs, I didn't care. I got my selfie and life was perfect!

 Tamara, I am FIERCE @YouAreFIERCE May 16, 2015

I don't want to be at the end of my life regretting that I didn't live the life I was meant to live
#ICanDoItEdmonton @DrWayneDyer

Me and Wayne Dyer at the "I Can Do It" conference in
Edmonton on May 18, 2015

I floated throughout the rest of the day with a renewed sense of purpose and knew that I couldn't put off writing the book anymore.

What I didn't know was that my biggest lesson in forgiveness was about to happen and completely change my mindset, once again.

The next day, Mastin Kipp took the stage. I had no idea who he was or what to expect from him so I didn't expect anything. His presence was large and charismatic, as he danced on stage to *Uptown Funk* by Mark Ronson featuring Bruno Mars. Mastin had the crowd on its feet. He talked about redemption and grace and love, but it wasn't until he had everyone do an exercise in forgiveness that something snapped inside of me. He told us to close our eyes and go back to a memory that caused us pain.

I went back to a dark place, one I thought I had walked away from and healed, one I never wanted to return to ever again. I went back to when I was 15 years old, lying on my bedroom floor and being kicked in the ribs by a monster in steel-toed boots and taking the worst beating I'd ever taken. I felt the pain and couldn't open my eyes to escape the memory. Tears streamed down my face, uncontrollably, and I was locked in that moment.

This time, instead of it being a dream, I was fully awake but forced to face the one demon I never could exorcise. I faced my stepdad and watched him through the eyes of a broken little girl. I felt myself leave that girl on the floor and watch the scene from a different perspective. I saw him hurt her, no remorse, his eyes blank with rage. I forced myself to catch my breath, taking control of the situation in my mind but my body was reacting in a completely different way.

The tears wouldn't stop and I could feel the sobs building up in my chest. I was afraid I was going to break down in the crowd of 2,000+ people and it took every ounce of self-control to keep my mouth shut. I went back to that scene, guided by Mastin's words and knowing I was safe.

I wanted to wrap my arms around that little girl and tell her it would be OK but I could only stand by and let the scene unfold. I knew the only way I could save her was to forgive him.

So I did.

In that moment, in a crowd of strangers and locked in a memory with only one way out, I forgave him. I let go of the hate, I let go of the pain and I let go of the hold he had on me.

I sat there with my head in my hands, silently weeping and feeling yet another chain release from my soul. My head hurt, my makeup was ruined and I was emotionally drained. So what does Mastin do? Asks us to turn to the person beside us and share our experience.

Uh, hell to the no, Mastin, I yelled at him in my mind. I got up and went to the bathroom, needing to compose myself and process what the hell had just happened to me.

Tamara, I am FIERCE @YouAreFIERCE   May 17, 2015

SUNUVA!!! I'd like to thank @MastinKipp for RUINING MY MAKEUP :'(what a powerful experience #ICanDoItEdmonton #tears #learnedalot

The "I Can Do It" conference was a life-changing experience for me in so many ways. I refocused on my book, I released that final anchor and understood the power of forgiveness, and I was finally ready to close the book on my past. The only reason it needs to be shared is to maybe, just maybe, give someone else hope that no matter what they're going through, they will get through it.

Life is a series of moments that change you, shape you, break you and make you who you are. Nothing – not your past, not your friends, not your family and definitely not your mistakes – defines you other than who you become as a result of it all.

All of the people who have been woven into your story were there to teach you something whether you wanted to learn it or not. This journey is like a *Choose Your Own Adventure* book with different options and different outcomes, but the entire story has been written by a greater power. If you can see the signs and follow the universe's lead, you can shortcut past the crap and go straight for the happiness you deserve.

We all have our demons, our stories and our baggage; it's what we choose to do with them that matters.

I choose to be FIERCE!

TAMARA PLANT

THE PROBLEM WITH ALL OF THIS

Surprise! I wasn't done! This is a sneak peek into the workbook you can download but this chapter also addresses a couple of the things I found sooooo very wrong with the self-empowerment kingdom during my healing journey.

We all want to improve ourselves. We attend the seminars, repost the affirmations, repeat the mantras and search for that elusive inner peace. We know what to do (light the candles, practice yoga, eat healthy, blah blah blah) but then you have a bad day and can't understand why you can't keep your cool when a series of little things makes lose your temper. Or you see someone snap a selfie and it makes you roll your eyes because that person is obviously narcissistic and self-absorbed and you would never do that but then you realize how judgemental that is and just sigh because you have to add that to your list of things to fix about yourself.

The journey towards ascension and becoming the best of your authentic self is a lifelong one that takes constant practice.

It's nice to aspire to reach the level of Zen that Wayne Dyer achieved (RIP good Sir!) where nothing fazes you and you see everything with love but the reality is that being human makes it extremely difficult to *not* react when your emotions are tested. During his speech at the "I Can Do It" conference, he mentioned how he would write all of these wonderful things but then his kids would call him out when he would lose his temper. Granted, that was 30-ish years ago but it's nice to know that even the people we aspire to be have struggled to get to where they are.

Shit happens.

Death, accidents, trauma, health issues, job stress, irritating colleagues, kids, marriage, life.

Sometimes it feels like you're being tested for some past karmic bullshit because why else would all of this stuff, and you just snap. You yell at your kids for leaving the bread on the counter, you swear at the driver who cuts you off because he's an asshole and you tweet a snarky comment to some celebrity, condemning them or judging what they wear.

Then you light your candle and take a deep breath and turn on your guided meditation from Doreen Virtue and all is well again.

Since I've been a student of positive thinking and spirituality, I've been drawn to various teachings and searching for words that speak to my soul. For me, it's difficult to automatically buy what someone is selling especially if I sense they are coming from a very egocentric place.

I have a really astute bullshit detector and I can see through almost any façade so it especially irks me when someone says all the right things but doesn't live what they preach. Or they spout their gospel of being light but never speak of their own darkness.

I have a real trigger point with that and yes, I'm working on it.

During my initial stages of seeking out messages of enlightenment, I was drawn to an author who motivates and speaks to success based on starting your day at 5 a.m. Since I'm up most mornings by 4 a.m. I was drawn to the message and bought into the ideas. I tweeted out the messages, jumped on the bandwagon and decided this author was the one I needed to follow because they had the answers I so desperately needed.

Halle-fucking-lujah!! I saw the light!

And then I went to a conference where that author was the keynote speaker.

I peeked over my rose coloured glasses during the speech and I started to see through the words directly to who they were coming from.

"My father said, 'When you were born, you cried and the world rejoiced. Live your life so that when you die, the world cries and you rejoice.'"

Uhm. I was pretty sure it wasn't your dad who SAID THAT, I thought to myself. It's a Cherokee proverb not some divine wisdom from your Pops, jackass.

I wondered to myself just how much of the sermon was coming from an authentic place in this person's life and exactly how many people were believing his bullshit. I also questioned why I bothered to listen to someone who couldn't offer me any indication of real experience on the subject of resilience.

Add another layer of jade to my already jaded personality and here we are. Four years after I saw said speaker, I have finally found what I was looking for and, just like Dorothy from *The Wizard of Oz*, it was always inside of me. I just had to tap my little red shoes and recognize that what I needed truly did lie within myself.

Along this yellow brick road of my journey, I have met a plethora of speakers and authors, all of varying styles and personalities and I've taken from them snippets of knowledge that has helped to rebuild my soul, stitching it together with their words of wisdom. There have been three types of teachers in my life: people like Wayne Dyer, Louise Hay and Deepak Chopra who have achieved a state of enlightenment that I can only aspire to.

There have been earth angels who have come into my life when I needed them the most whether it was a friend who has come and gone or a mentor who believed in me when no one else did and I sure as hell couldn't see anything good about myself, or a stranger with a kind word when I needed it the most.

And then there have been the teachers who have come into my life causing me pain, physically, emotionally and spiritually. I have more of those teachers than anything else and as many scars as I bear from their lessons, they were the most valuable teachers of all. All of these people entered my life as soul mates, the Red String of Fate.

Let's pause for a moment and evaluate the teachers in your life.

If you look back on your journey, take a look at the people who have betrayed you, lied to you, hurt you in some way whether it was a family member or a stranger. What did you learn from those people? Did you continually allow them to cause you pain or drag you down to their level of consciousness or did you eventually learn the lessons and cut them out of your life? What impact did they have on where you are now and how you treat others? What did you take from your time with them? What did you leave?

Teachers come in all sizes, shapes, colours and forms. They are brought into our life through a series of events, usually when we least expect it and always when we need them the most. The teachers we seek out are generally when we're on our healing journey, when we're looking for guidance, strength and transformation.

So how do you choose a teacher? I wish I could give you a cookie cutter template that would work for everyone but the truth is that you have to trust yourself.

Tip #1: Be open to receiving the message. What you need to learn will come to you from the most unexpected sources; movies, songs, billboards, a magazine ad, twitter, a friend, a stranger and so on and so on. If you're not willing to hear or see the message, the same thing will be put in front of you a hundred times until you are ready and then it will be the biggest AHA moment of your life. You'll wonder why you never saw it before.

Tip #2 - What do you already "know?"

I had a conversation on Twitter with someone who refused to believe that people stay in your life for a reason, even if you can't stand them. I told him they were there until you learned the lesson you needed to learn and could simply release them from your immediate bubble.

"No. There are people like my ex who are in my life forever. Doesn't matter that I want her gone, she's always going to be there because of our kids."

I won't try to convince anyone of anything, especially in 140 characters because it's exhausting and draining so I let it go.

The fact is that once you learn the lesson from the person who is in your life that you can't stand, ex or not, you can release those harsh feelings and go on with your life, reclaiming your power and letting go of that toxic energy.

A month later, I was scrolling through Facebook when BAM! I saw this quote:

"Nothing will ever go away until it has taught us what we need to know."
~ Pema Chödrön

Hmmmm, I thought. Who is this Pema person and why is she swiping my awesome wisdom? I Googled her and discovered this description on her website: "Beloved Buddhist teacher, author, nun and mother, Pema Chödrön has inspired millions of people from around the world who have been touched by her example and message of practicing peace in these turbulent times."

Well, fuck. There went my idea that all of my infinite wisdom that I had come by naturally was original, I laughed to myself. Obviously I knew I wasn't going to be blowing the minds of people with my personal discoveries. I had done more inner work by reflecting, contemplating and thinking out loud than looking for answers from anyone else but finding out that what I found out through experience was actually validated by a world-renowned Buddhist teacher, was pretty cool.

I bet Pema never dropped an F-bomb, though, I thought. That's OK, I don't want to be twinsies I just like the idea that my ideas are already being preached by people who are highly respected and pretty badass in their own right.

Ask yourself what you intuitively know for certain and then write it down. If it's something that you firmly believe but were never taught, it's divine wisdom. Maybe you're not the only person who has thought it and it's validated by a so-called expert. I don't believe you need anyone to back up what you believe in. You don't need the masses to jump on the bandwagon for your beliefs but it is pretty cool when you find your people and can discuss common beliefs.

So what do you know for certain?

_____
_____
_____
_____
_____
_____
_____
_____

Step 3 - Understand that what you believe is your truth.

I used to intentionally steered clear of motivational speakers and authors because some of their stuff seemed like artificial crap. A friend told me she was in a spiritual shop and after her purchase, the cashier put his hand on hers and said, *"If you're not within, you're without."*

"What the hell?" I said, confused. "He said what?"

152

"If you're not within, you're without," she replied. "Isn't that the most amazing thing you've ever heard?"

"BAHAHAHAHAHAHAHAHAHHAHAHAHAHHAHAA HHAH!"

She sneered at me, offended that I wasn't as deeply affected by the quote as she was but the truth was, it sounded ridiculous.

"He may as well have quoted Yoda, for fuck sakes," I said.

Yeah, we're not friends anymore because I was an arrogant jackass. It was disrespectful of me to dismiss her light bulb moment as something that was lame and fluffy. Who am I to judge someone's path?

I'm all for whatever you need to be inspired by, regardless of where the message comes from, but I need my inspiration to be slightly looser and less uptight. Of course it depends on my mood, too. There have been times when I've seen beautiful, soul-stirring messages that have brought me to tears, sobbing at how they resonated with me, as those words gently removed a brick or two from the walls I had built up around me.

What works for me won't work for someone else. That's the point of this whole book. Take what works, what resonates and what gives you a lightbulb moment then discard what doesn't suit you. I have yet to find one author/teacher who I 100 per cent agree with.

Have you ever reacted negatively to someone else's belief system? Own it, remember. If you have, don't beat yourself up over it. What can you learn from the experience? How do you feel about your reaction now? Are you more tolerant?

_____

_____

_____

For the complete workbook and the bonus chapter, please visit YouAreFIERCE.com/thebook.

If you're on Twitter, send me your thoughts or feel free to ask questions @YouAreFIERCE using #stupidthings

I am grateful that you took the time to get to know me. The best of who I am recognizes the best in who you are.

Much love and light on your journey, wherever you may be.

ABOUT THE AUTHOR

Tamara Plant is the founder of YouAreFIERCE.com, a community built on inspiring, elevating and connecting people who want to purge the negativity in their lives. She offers workshops on how to live your own inspired life and can often be found tweeting about coffee, her ridiculously (and possibly delusional) long list of Hollywood boyfriends, *The Walking Dead* and wine. Oh, and once she tweeted with S.E. Hinton while watching *The Outsiders*. It was by far the coolest experience of her life.

55268314R00100

Made in the USA
Charleston, SC
25 April 2016